MEMOIRS OF AN UNSUNG WARRIOR

Doma Panduranga Reddy

ISBN 979-8-89363-299-6

The Dedication of the Book to Telangana Martyrs (students and youth) who sacrificed their precious Lives for Separate Telangana State!!!

We, the people of Telangana place on
record with high admiration, appreciation,
acknowledgement and sincere gratitude to
Smt. Sonia Gandhi ji
for making Telangana, the 29th Indian State

DOWN THE MEMORY LANE
(INDEX)

1. SPEAKING FROM MY HEART

The erstwhile Hyderabad state was under supression by various rulers for a long time by Asaf Jahi dynasty and intruders like people from Andhra region for over 6 decades.

The development of Hyderabad state was decimal as Andhra rulers have completely neglected Telangana area in all aspects.

This gave rise to a movement for seperate statehood by the people of Telangana as early as 1969 but got fizzled out due to political reasons. Later once again in 2001 the peoples' movement primarily lead by youth and students picked up momentum at a large scale, withouit violence but pity that a few hundred youth immolised themselves for pressing their demands.

I was one among those warriors participating, guiding and leading, the Movement. Telangana Development Forum - India (TDF - India) is a sister organisation of TDF - USA with sole objective of educating masses and intellectuals on the need for seperate Telangana and to establish a vision document for Telangana and also dispute the wrong perceptions of Sri Krishna Committee appointed by the Government for fact finding.

The Movement has been an important part of my life apart from many accomplishments in work and service and it became of platform to place my inner feelings out of my heart to the people of my beloved state Telangana.

Hence this booklet.

Place : Hyderabad
Date :

- D.P.Reddy

2. THE BEGINNING!

Born as 2nd son to Sri DOMA Bheem Reddy / Smt. Manemma couple in a tiny village Pathoor of erstwhile Hyderabad and persent Vikarabad district in 1946.

My father had about 100 acres (40.50 hectars) of land in our village and had a very good name and reputation in the village and surrounding areas. As a Sarpanch, (Head of the village elected by people) he was instrumental in resolving the villagers' issues, conflicts and had a good rapport with government officials too.

My earlier education up to 3rd standard started in the village itself with a Khanigi (Private) teacher Azimuddin Saheb. He taught us alphabets on the sand in the beginning and on the slate later.

After successful completion of 3rd standard in my village, my father admitted me in Zilla Parishad High School (ZPHS) Vikarabad, a small town near to my village in the 4th class. Primary education infact was the foundation for further higher education. My brother and 2 uncles were also studying in the same school at Vikarabad.

I used to recite Telugu poems of Vemana, Krishna and Sumati Satakams (a sataka means 100 poems) without looking in to books. Teachers used to encourage me to continue the skill of getting them by heart and also to help other students to do the same.

My father rented a house in Vikarabad. A group of 10 persons stayed together including my 2 uncles and 1 brother. We all were reading in the light of a lantern as there was no power those days in small places.

My duty was to wash and clean the utensils. During examinations, we were studying under the street lights. During my High School days only street lights were connected with electricity. Several great national leaders in our country had studied under street lights.

We used to fetch firewood for cooking from nearby Ananthagiri forest which is close to Vikarabad town. During weekends we were visiting our village Pathoor by foot as there was no tranposrtation at that time.

On the way to our village, we were drinking water from "Chelima" - a small stream on the ground and the water used to be pure and sweet.

In the holidays we were helping the family in agricultural activities like moving manure to fields by bullock carts, seed crushing and seeds collection, jaggery making, etc. It was a very interesting activity in the holidays and was the main professional activities of a farmer's family.

Ladies in the house were busy 2-3 hours in the morning and 2-3 hours in the evening to make Jowar Roti (bread) for the family members and servants to serve them when they return from the fields after work.

My father used to frequent Vikarabad to check our welfare and used to bring various eatables and home made snacks. Apart from delicious taste, they contained my mother's love and affection for us.

Our family had, a rare phenomenon of high level children education not only in our village but in entire district which made my parents feel proud of us. It was all due to the importance given to education by my father.

I passsed the 10th Class examination in 1st rank out of 58 students.

Our teachers in the school were all non-graduates except Head Master but their dedication to teaching was inspirational. At that time teachers' salaries were very low, Rs. 300 to Rs. 700 per month but their commitment and contribution was very high which is the reverse case in present day faculty.

Up to high school, the medium of instruction was in Telugu which is our mother tongue. I got 96 marks in Telugu exams, but only 40 marks in English. Our Telugu State was never under British rule.

There used to be several festivities and entertainment programs like Bhagothalu all night by artists who go village to village and perform their arts.

Bathukamma celebration of women for ten days, in some times during October performed collectively and later the diety will be immersed in a tank.

One of such important festival is Dussehra also called as Vijaya Dasami or Durgaastami. Village elders generally go to write a pledge to God believing that it will   help in prosperity sitting under Spurge tree (Jammi Chettu). For Muslims, Peerlapanduga was very auspeciouis but even Hindus used to join in their festivities. There was perfect religious tolerance in those days.

We used to go for swimming in Mella Baavi (Well) during the summer holidays, swimming was an interesting sport, taking AMBALI (Ragi malt) after coming home after swimming.

Every Saturday evening Bhajan was in our home and at Hanuman temple too.

I used to join my father to recite Bhagavatham for 7 days. Weddings were another happy occasion, where all relatives meet and greet .

Common dishes in weddings were Annam (Rice), Pappu, Thokku, Poorilu, Polelu, Boondi and Laddu, etc.,

Major games were Kabaddi, Gilli Dandi and Football, etc., in schools and villages specially during summary holidays.

Water to the fields was fetched from deep wells pulled by bullocks by a chain system.

In the village people used to call one another by assumed relationship and never by name. Affectionate acts with villagers calling them (Mama, Atha, Akka, Anna, Chicha, Pinni, Thammi, Chelli etc.)

Reading all types of books was a summer pass time..

There was NO electricity initially in villages and towns : hence we were using Kerosene lamps or oil lamps for regular works and studies too.

Playing Cards (Pathalu) was a pastime in holidays : Game 304 or Beet - Saat, Rummy, etc., but without any money or betting!

There were NO toilets at that time and community defecating outside village was a practcie .

Our main food was Jonna Rottelu (Jowar Roti) Korra Annamu (Fox millets rice) almost every day for family members as well as servants too.

As my father was a very religious person, our family was vegetarian and no smoking or drinking was allowed. After going abroad, I started eating non-veg food with a friend's force ! No alcohol in our family even today.

Early days of life between pathoor and Vikarabad was memorable and laid strong foundation to be successful in the later years.

3. FIRST MOVES OF A MOVEMENT

As a final year engineering student, I visited several near by villages of Vikarabad, our native place with about 25-30 students / youth to educate the rural people about the injustice done by Andhra rulers to Telangana and the need for demanding a separate state.

In 1969 the 1st wave of movement for seperate state was heralded by Telangana Praja Samithi headed by Dr. M. Chenna Reddy. In those days there used to be only public radio in the village in Grama Panchayat Office with a loud speaker and that was the only source of communication to know the news.

During the 1st phase / wave of agitation for a seperate statehood almost 370 students were brutally killed by Government, to suppress the demand for separte statehood.

Then there were assembly elections.

Police arrested us in Vikarabad Cross Roads when we took a rally and were protesting the injustices done to Telangana. Police took us to Hyderabad and kept us in a temporary jail. Then released from Jail after three weeks after C.M. Brahmandha Reddy's resignation.

I had particiapted in the Telangana Praja Samithi (TPS) assembly election campaign in Siddipet in favour of Mr. Madan Mohan a leading activist of Telangana Movement.

Telangana Praja Samithi won 10 out of 14 Loksabha seats in the elections. Smt. Indira Gandhi of Indian National Congress swept the polls with absolute majority and became the Prime Minister of India once again.

At that time there was no communication like TVs, Internet, Fb, Twitter, Whatsapp, etc., We used to listen to Radio news only, at village Panchayat Offices/ Schools, etc., BBC also was giving Telangana News on it's broadcast. In the 1969 T-Movement, there were many activists - employees and students etc., participated voluntarily. The government headed by Mr. K. Brahmananda Reddy   killed about 370 students/ youth in police firing.

4. GLIMPSES OF APATHY TELANGANA MOVEMENT

I had keen interest in the development of the Telangana Movement and was prepared for any kind of consequence.

Across Hyderabad, river Musi flows but as it was not looked after well by the Government and it became a garbage tank and was polluted heavily. The video clip attached will explain the grave situation of the Musi river.

The pollution levels were so high that mothers were not in a position to feed their babies as the breast milk is contaminated with toxic materials. The incidence of skin diseases, cancer, miscarriages and abortions were very high. Even the Supreme Court judgments could not solace the locals as industrialists colluded with Pollution Control Board officials using political/ bureaucratic power.

The surrounding areas of beautiful Hyderabad have become the dumpyards for industrial effluents threatening the lives and health of people there. An extreme example for this is RAMKY -a solid waste management company from ("Seemandhra is a region in the state of Andhra Pradesh, India), which was illegally bringing and dumping industrial wastes not only from Telangana but also from Andhra area.

Our history stands witness to point out that from 1324 to 1948 - the Telangana region was ruled by five muslim dynasties. During these 624 years Telanganaites had untold hardship, gross neglect and were treated as secondary citizens. Telangana people never had the opportunity to enjoy freedom, rights and respect.

5. KEY ISSUES BEHIND THE DEMERGER DEMAND

- A Representation by me.

My SKC Report - by D.P.Reddy, T.DF - India.

A) Irrigation and Power

Though Telangana has 70% catchment area of Krishna and Godavari rivers, only 5 lakh acres out of 35 lakh acres, were getting irrigated. (1 hectare = 2.471 acres).

Under Jalayagnam scheme several projects were taken up in Telangana area with huge budgets but even after five years not a single acre of land got water in Telangana.

The major beneficiaries of Jalayagnam were Andhra capitalists/contractors who were siphoning government's money with the help of politicians and bureaucrats for development of their region. Most of politicians turned as contractors and businessmen and were opposing Telangana State formation for their selfish motives.

There were many vital irrigation projects of Telangana that were willfully neglected by the Andhra rulers. A classic example is, that of the Sriram Sagar project of Nizamabad district which has been kept in cold storage for the last 50 years.

Power Purchase Agreements [PPA] initiated by Chandrababu Naidu and continued by his successor Sri Y.S. Rajasekhar Reddy a boon to these Andhra capitalists to make money illegally. Like the Jalayagnam contractors, these PPA contractors were also opposing Telangana formation as they fear losing of their regular illegal income.

B) Education & Employment :

Telangana accounts for about 42% of the area and population in undivided Andhra Pradesh. As per fair share principle, Telanganites must get 42% in education and employment opportunities. Telangana share never crossed 10% in secretariat and similar was the case with other departments. The fact that no person from Telangana was appointed as Advocate General testifies this.

One may be surprised that my native Ranga Reddy district, the surrounding district of Hyderabad, does not have a single government degree college even today. The budget for education of Guntur district of Andhra Region alone is much higher than all the nine Telangana districts excluding Hyderabad city.

C) Language, History and Culture :

Telangana dialect was despised and humiliated in the name of standard language. Whereas the so-called Standard language was spoken in two districts, but the Telangana dialect was spoken in 10 districts. Text books of schools and colleges contain the Andhra dialect so are the official documents of the government thus belittling the Telangana dialect. Telangana dialect was looked down and used for characters of villains, comedians in movies, TV shows and radio programmes which was hurting the sentiments and feelings of Telanganites.

Similarly Telangana history and culture did not get the adequate attention and respect of the government. Andhra bureaucracy was not giving prominence to archaeological and historical places of Telangana with a cultural heritage of 5000 years. Through these acts, successive Andhra rulers are seriously hurting the sentiments of 4 Crore (40 million) Telangana people which was also a root cause for demanding a separate state.

D) Biased Media:

Electronic and print media in Andhra Pradesh was controlled by Andhra capitalists. Even the film industry which got land and other facilities at cheaper rates in Telangana was controlled by a handful of Andhra land lords . These media tycoons are giving a false picture of the present Telangana Movement and are opposing the formation of Telangana State to continue their dominance.

E) Backwardness in Telangana districts :

Every Telangana district was plagued by some problem or the other. HMTV conducted 16 LIVE programmes [out of which 7 were in Telangana] to know the pulse and problems of the people and why they want a separate state. One should watch all these LIVE programmes of HMTV to understand the core issues.

Major issues of the Telangana districts are listed below:

➢ Land grabbing.

➢ Pollution.

➢ Traffic congestion,

➢ Lack of adequate civic amenities

➢ Fluorosis content in drinking water

➢ Migration and starvation for livelyhood.

➢ Encroachment of tribal lands

➢ Migration to Gulf countries and miserable life there.

- ➢ Spread of tropical diseases, unhygeinic living places for tribals.

- ➢ Grabbing of tribal lands and inundation of tribal villages in the name of Polavaram project.

- ➢ Countless suicides of handloom workers in Karimnagar and the pathetic plight of Beedi workers.

Are we in a democratic country?

After graduating in B.Tech Chemical Engineering from Osmania University in 1969 and M.Tech from Regional Engineering College, Warangal in 1971 I had worked in India and abroad for over 3 decades and had the opportunity of traveling worldwide from USA to Far East and from Europe to Middle East. I experienced different forms of governments - kingdoms in Iran, military dictatorships in Nigeria and democratic setups in the USA/UK and other countries. But nowhere in the world did I see the suppression of democratic aspirations of people as was done in case of Telangana for the last 54 years. Literally after this the democracy was under peril. After undergoing this injustice for so long by the people of Telangana, I really doubt whether India is a democratic country, and whether we are living in a democratic setup? India and USA are supposed to be the largest democracies of the world, but see the fate of Telanganites in democratic India!!! And adding insult to injury Telangananites were treated as secondary citizens in their own homeland.

On 7th December 2009, all the political parties in the Legislative Assembly of A.P passed a unanimous resolution on Telangana under the chairmanship of Chief Minister Rosaiah in support of separate state. Based on this, the Hon. Home

Minister of India Sri P.Chidambaram on 9th December, 2009 announced that the process of formation of Telangana will be initiated and asked K. Chandra Sekhar Rao who was on indefinite fast to withdraw his hunger strike. Formation of Telangana was also supported by the opposition party BJP and other political parties in the Parliament.

Within hours of the Home Minister's statement on Telangana, Seemandhra MLAs and MPs have shown their true colours and started tendering mass resignations opposing the Telangana formation.

Andhra leaders within hours scuttled the dreams of Telanganites to have their own State. It was strange to note that major political parties of Andhra Pradesh gave two contradictory reports to the Sri Krishna Committee – favouring and opposing Telangana.

Deployment of Greyhounds, CRPF,SPF battalions and brutal lathi charge on the students in Osmania University (OU) campus was gross violation of human rights and the Union Government was held responsible and answerable. Despite the Home Minister announced the withdrawal of the cases against O.U Students on 9th Dec 2009, Around 30-40 cases against some students, those were still kept active for a long time.

UPA government under the chairmanship of Sonia Gandhi, Prime Minister Manmohan Singh and Home Minister Chidambaram should have been felt ashamed of delaying the process of forming Telangana State under the pressure tactics of Andhra lobby with their money and muscle power. In such a situation can we confidently say that Democracy was there and will be there in India ?.   The UPA Government totally and unconditionally surrendered to the Andhra lobby and made Telanganites to suffer eternally?

After the announcement of Home Minister Sri. P.Chidambaram on Telangana State initiation process on 9th Dec 2009, National and International media declared Telangana as the 29th state of India.

The Indian Government was shameless and not even thought of how they will answer the international community / diplomats and media for delaying the formation of Telangana - the 29th State of India. Meanwhile the Government has appointed a fact finding committee headed by Justice Sri Krishna only to buy time and as delaying tactics. Justice Sri Krishna Committee term was extended till the year end and thus perpetuating the misery of innocent Telangana people. Any democratic country in the world - except maybe our great India under the UPA Government can do this type of undemocratic practice.

Due to the delay in the formation of Telangana State and the provocative statements of Andhra leaders, the disgusted students/youth resorted to sacrificing their lives in the name of Telangana. Over 270 persons committed suicide in this phase of Telangana movement. During 1969 Telangana agitation more than 370 persons died in police firing.

Our concern was how many more lives of Telangana youth the Indian government want to take before declaring the Telangana State?

It was ignoble on the part of the Indian government who dismissed all the democratic norms and disowned their own statements.

We humbly submitted to the Sri Krishna Committee to respect the aspirations of people of Telangana and requested to give a favourable report for the formation of Telangana State.

The Illegal transactions of land dealings as well as Jalayagnam commission money were pumped into Hyderabad real estate business and thus politicians/ business barons made tonnes of illegal money. Hyderabad and Telangana became the money bank for Andhrites.

During the 7th Asaf Jahi Mir Osman Ali Khan era Hyderabad was the FOURTH largest city in India and in 2009 it became the FIFTH largest. Nizam was the richest person of the world, with his photo on the cover page of TIME magazine of 1937.

The Nizam brought glory to Hyderabad city but Andhras spoiled it and made Hyderabad a SCAM CITY due to several scams SATYAM & MAYTAS, Krushi Bank, Prudential Bank, Nagarjuna Finance, Charminar Bank and several other Real Estate Scams like Lanco Hills of Lagadapati Rajagopal. Despite all this, Hyderabad is being preferred by national and international IT and Software giants like TCS, Infosys, Wipro, Microsoft, IBM, Dell, Google, Oracle etc.

Hyderabad is the major producer and exporter of chemicals and pharmaceuticals in the country and it is also an international medical center with well known corporate hospitals.

Now these capitalists and scamsters don't want to leave Hyderabad and are opposing Telangana state formation demanding Hyderabad be made as a Union Territory.

Hyderabad is an integral part of Telangana and without Hyderabad the Telangana state will be like a body without a head!!!

The share of education funding for Telangana ranges from 9.86% in Government aided primary schools to 37.85% in Government Degree Colleges. The above nubers include the expenditure in Hyderabad. Budget allocation to Telangana was generally less than 1/3 of the total Andhra pradesh budget. In most years funds allocated to Telangana were never spent. Since 1956 Andhra Pradesh Government estabished 11 new medical colleges in the state. 8 were in Seemandhra, 3 were in Telangana. Telangana was not compensated for loss of opportunity becasue of inward migration of lot of students from Seemandhra to Hyderabad. Accordiong to Prof. Jayashanker, The father of Telangana movement only 20% of the Government employees less than 10% in secretariate, less than 5% as department heads of Andhra Pradesh Government were from Telangana. No Chief Minister was for more than 2½ years from Telangana, total 6½ years from Telangana out of 50 Years.

A comprehensive detail of Telangana Movement as was submitted to Sri Krishna Committee by the President of Telangana Development Forum - India Mr. D.P. Reddy.

The Hyderabad State had been longing for democracy and rule of law for many many years. Their hopes got boosted with the Police Action of 1948 when Hyderabad State was annexed with Indian Union. But their dreams were short-lived as the Telangana region was forcefully merged with Andhra State in 1956 against the recommendation of the first SRC. Even the then Prime Minister Jawaharlal Nehru opined that the demand for Vishalandra 'bore a tint of expansionist imperialism' (*Indian Express October 17, 1953*). People of Telangana, who were under the Nizam's rule, were innocent, suppressed, and backward with little education and that too in Urdu medium. Whereas, Andhras were English educated, rich, clever and were under British rule.

Starting with 1953, Telangana saw the constitution of eight committees and commissions to study the demand for separate State of Telangana and other issues related to it. People of Telangana got fed up with these committees and commissions as none of the recommendations favourable to Telangana were implemented. The committees included:

Fazal Ali Commission (First SRC) (1953-55), Lalith Committee (1969), Bhargava Committee (1969), Jaya Bharath Reddy Committee (1985), House Committee on G.O 610 (2001), Girglani Committee (2003), Pranab Mukherjee Committee (2004) and K.Rosaiah Committee (2009).

Dishonouring the recommendations of these committees was in addition to the violation of the promises given in various agreements, legislations, government orders and formulas.

Keeping all these facts in mind, with strong protest we submitted a report to the Justice Sri Krishna Committee (9th committee on Telangana) for the demerger of Telangana as Telangana was an independent State before the merger and it must be so treated by the Justice Srikrishna Committee (SKC).

We were also objected to the 1st point of SKC Terms of Reference [ToR] , as it seeks to take the opinion of the Andhra region which is not necessary. Sri Krishna Committee's main focus should be on a separate Telangana State and for this, it should take the opinion of the Telangana people only.

After all, why will the oppressors, who got immensely benefited in integrated Andhra Pradesh, agree for separate Telangana State?

Merger or demerger - Hyderabad is the focal point

Telangana people opposed the merger in 1956, but the Andhra lobby manipulated Delhi and forced Telangana leaders for the merger with certain conditions as espoused in Gentlemen's Agreement. After separating from composite Madras State in 1953, Andhra State operated from Kurnool in tents and without proper accommodation for offices like Assembly, Secretariat and shelter for Government employees and MLA's etc. Hence Andhra leaders eyed Hyderabad as it was a beautiful city in all aspects to provide offices, infrastructure and modern living facilities.

Hyderabad was the main reason to merge Telangana with Andhra to form Andhra Pradesh in 1956, in the name of common language i.e. Telugu and now in 2009-10 they are opposing the demerger of Telangana citing Hyderabad and its development by them which is not at all a fact and whatever development done was in Seemandhra by syphoning money from Hyderabad.

Here's what India Today magazine says

"One of the reasons for the Telangana stir to spin out of control with almost the entire state edging towards near-paralysis was the fear that Hyderabad may be transferred to the new state. Scores of powerful politicians who have sizable business interests in Hyderabad and Telangana, along with real estate sharks allegedly abetted the anti-Telangana fire."

People like Lagadapati Rajgopal was championing the cause of a United Andhra Pradesh because he happens to own the costliest real-estate project in Hyderabad. Similarly several other politicians-turned-businessmen from Seemandhra region who have interests in Power Purchase Agreements and Jalayagnam commissions have amassed illegal wealth with patronage from ruling classes and bureaucrats. These opponents of Telangana State fear

that their misdeeds would be exposed if the new state is formed.

As per Gentlemen's Agreement of 1956, Telangana lands should not be bought by non-Telanganites; and for other purposes also they have to take permission from Telangana Regional Committee (TRC). But successive governments of Andhra-dominated rulers have amended the laws and non-Telanganites purchased valuable lands in and around Hyderabad as well as fertile lands in Telangana districts at throw-away prices.

Nizam kept about 10% of the lands in his kingdom to meet personal expenditure. This land, known as Sarf-E-Khas extended to about 1,20,000 acres. The areas surrounding Hyderabad was known as Atraf-E-Balda and it consisted of approximately 5,00,000 acres.

After Police Action in September 1948, most of this land was transferred to the Hyderabad State and then, post merger of Telangana region with Andhra state in 1956 all this land was inherited by Andhra Pradesh government. These same lands of Nizams as well as assigned lands, temple lands and wakf lands were illegally transferred to Andhra capitalists by Chandrababu Naidu and YSR Governments from 1999 to 2009.

The illegal transactions of land dealings as well as Jalayagnam commission money were pumped into Hyderabad real estate business and thus politicians/business barons made tonnes of illegal money.

The Nizam brought glory to Hyderabad city but Andhras spoiled it and made Hyderabad a SCAM CITY due to several scams - SATYAM & MAYTAS, Krushi Bank, Prudential Bank, Nagarjuna Finance, Charminar Bank and several other Real

Estate Scams like Lanco Hills of Lagadapati Rajagopal. Despite all this, Hyderabad is being preferred by national and international IT and Software giants like TCS, Infosys, Wipro, Microsoft, IBM, Dell, Google,Oracle etc.

Hyderabad is the major producer and exporter of chemicals and pharmaceuticals in the world and it is also an international medical center with well known corporate hospitals.

Now these capitalists and scamsters don't want to leave Hyderabad and are opposing Telangana state formation demanding Hyderabad be made as a Union Territory.

Hyderabad is an integral part of Telangana and without Hyderabad the Telangana state will be like a body without a head!!!

Industries and Pollution:

The major industries of Telangana like Nizam Sugar Factory, PragaTools, Azamjahi Mills, DBR Mills etc. were slowly and systematically made sick and were closed, throwing lakhs of workers to the streets. Similarly many of the public sector industries like IDPL, Allwyn, HMT Bearings etc. were also closed down and Andhra rulers conspired to convert them into real estate ventures like malls, hotels etc.

Several Andhra entrepreneurs established Drug and Chemical industries in and around Hyderabad and today almost all the Telangana districts are under the blanket of pollution. These Andhra entrepreneurs benefitted from the government incentives and entered into FORBES and FORTUNE billionaires list but never preferred locals for employment in their industries. Thus Telangana got a pollution ridden environment in return for the industry-

friendly environment it offered. Moreover, with the levels of pollution that exist today and the consequent restrictions Telangana entrepreneurs are deprived of their right to setup industries in their own region even NOW and in FUTURE.

The Musi river which was catering to the drinking water needs before merger got polluted completely with industrial wastes, toxic chemicals etc., all along its way from Patanchervu to Suryapet - a stretch of about 160 kms.

The following video clearly explains the grave & alarming situation of Musi river pollution.

http://www.youtube. com/watch? v=RR3QRDYs3cg

The pollution levels are so high that mothers are not in a position to feed their babies as the breast milk is contaminated with toxic materials. The incidence of skin diseases, cancer, miscarriages and abortions is very high. Even the Supreme Court judgments could not solace the locals and as industrialists colluded with PCB officials using political/ bureaucratic power.

The surrounding areas of Hyderabad have become the dumpyards for industrial effluents threatening the lives and health of people there. An extreme example for this is RAMKY —a solid waste management company from Seemandhra — which is illegally bringing and dumping industrial wastes not only from Telangana but also from Andhra area.

Can we confidently say that Democracy is working in India after the UPA government surrendered to the Andhra lobby and made Telanganites to suffer further?

After the announcement of Home Minister Sri. P.Chidambaram on Telangana State initiation process on 9th Dec 2009, National & International media declared Telangana as the 29th state of India.

Please find the news links from International media that talk about Telangana being the 29th state of India.

BBC

http://news.bbc.co.uk/2/hi/south_asia/8405146.stm

The Age

http://www.theage.com.au/world/india-to-set-up-its-29th-state-20091211-kmk0.html

Los Angeles Times

http://articles.latimes.com/2009/dec/12/world/la-fg-india-states12-2009dec12

Al Jajeera

http://english.aljazeera.net/news/asia/2009/12/20091210125953637704.html

Reuters

http://www.reuters.com/article/idUSDEL31450420091210

Wall Street Journal

MSN

We want to know from the Indian government how they will answer the international community/diplomats and media for delaying the formation of Telangana - the 29th State of India - by appointing Justice Sri Krishna Committee whose term Is till the year end and thus perpetuating the misery of innocent Telangana people. Any democratic country in the world – except maybe our great India under the UPA government - can do this type of undemocratic practice.

Due to the delay in the formation of Telangana State and the provocative statements of Andhra leaders, disgusted and emotional students/youth are sacrificing their lives in the name of Telangana. Till date, over 270 persons committed suicide in this phase of Telangana movement. During 1969 Telangana agitation more than 370 persons died in police firing.

How many more lives of Telangana youth the Indian government want to take before declaring the Telangana State?

It will be a shame to India — its public representatives in particular and people in general.

Hence I humbly submit to the Sri Krishna Committee to respect the aspirations of people of Telangana and request to give a favourable report for the formation of Telangana State.

Thanking You.

D. Panduranga Reddy

Founder, Telangana Rural Youth (TRY) Foundation

201, Pallavi Residency, H.No. 12-13-662,

Nagarjuna Nagar

Street 14, Lane 1, Tarnaka

Secunderabad – 500017. Phone: 09348877474

Email: dpreddy77@gmail.com

6 : MY ROLE IN TDF FOR TELANGANA MOVEMENT - SUMMARY

1919	:	Nizam issued Farmana to implement MULKI RULE [Employment for Locals only]
17th Sept 1948	:	Hyderabad state got Freedom even though India became Independent on 15th Aug 1947.
1952 1st	:	General Elections and Late. Sri Burgula Ramakrishna Rao as 1st Chief Minister (CM) of Hyderabad State
3rd Sep 1952	:	Non Mulki/Idli-Sambar Go Back, Gongura go back Agitation and 7 students died in Police firing @ CITY COLLEGE Hyderabad.
1st Oct 1953	:	Separate Andhra State formation [from Madras] with Kurnool as Capital
		Fazal Ali SRC Commission recommonding Telangana on Sep16th was started by students/ employees initially, but later Telangana Praja Samithi [TPS] under the leadership of Dr.M.Channa Reddy.
1971	:	General Elections TPS won 11 out of 14 MP seats: across India INC under Indira Gandhi won with comfortable majority in the Parliament. With brute majority in the

Parliament and Hyderabad case in UN,Indira Gandhi offered alternatives to Telangana instead of aSeparate State.

21st Sep1973 : With Jai Andhra and Jai Telangana Agitations Indira Gandhi announced 6-Point Formula by which Mulki Rules and Telangana Regional Committees were abolished.

2000 : 41 Congress MLA s representation to Sonia Gandhi Demanding Separate Telangana State.

2004 Feb : Telangana Vidyavanthula Vedika [TVV] formation with Kodandram, Mallepalli etc.,

7th Jun 2004 : TELANGANA in President Address in the Parliament.

8th Jan 2005 : Pranab Mukherji Committee on Telangana.

7th Dec 2007 : KCR win with 2 Lakhs majority in K.Nagar Bye-Election.

29th Nov 2009 : KCR's indefinite Hunger Strike for Telangana: Srikantha Chary Suicide attempt.

7th Dec 2009 : All Party Meeting under the Presidentship of CM Rosaiah decides that there is NO OBJECTION for Telangana State Creation.

| 9th Dec 2009 | : | Initiation of Telangana announcement by Home Minister Chidambaram as Sonia's Birthday Gift. |

SEQUENCE OF EVENTS

23rd Dec 2009	:	Second announcement by Chidambaram for more interactions with political parties and organisations etc.,
24th Dec2009	:	TJAC formation with political parties and organisations and Prof Kodandaram as Convenor TJAC.BANDH call by TJAC
30th Dec 2019	:	8 parties invited by central Govt for discussion on Telangana
1st Jan2010	:	Telangana Vidyarthi Garjana in OU
5th Jan 2010	:	All party meeting in Delhi on Telangana: Rail Roko, Vanta Vaarpu etc in Telangana 28th Jan 2010
		Sri Krishna Committee on Telangana : Announcement by Chidambaram from Delhi
3rd Feb 2010	:	Justice Sri Krishna Committee with 5 members announced
20th Feb 2010	:	Assembly Muttadi by OU Students JAC: Yadaiah's Suicide and Demise in OU campus
16th & 31st Mar 2010	:	Newyork Times special story on Suicides/ Sacrifices for Telangana 9th Dec2010 BJP DHARNA in Delhi for Telangana.

30th Dec 2010	:	SKC Report to GoI by SriKrishna Committee on Telangana.
16th Dec 2010	:	TRS MAHA GARJANA with 25 Lakhs people in Warangal.
1st Mar 2011	:	RAIL ROKO
10th Mar 2011	:	MILLION MARCH on Tankbund Hyderabad
19th Jun 2011	:	VANTA- VAARPU [Cooking on the Road] for Telangana
21st Jun2011	:	Demise of Prof Jayashanker
22nd Jul 2011	:	TJAC Telangana BANDH
21st Sep 2012	:	Demise of Konda Laxman Bapuji
30th Sep2012	:	TJAC Telangana March/Sagara Haaram
2nd Oct 2012	:	TJAC Mouna Deeksha @ Bapu Ghat
28th Dec 2012	:	Telangana in a Month -Shinde in All Party Meet in Delhi
27th Jan 2013	:	TJAC Samara Deeksha
21st Mar 2013	:	TJAC Sadak BANDH success
27th Apr 2013	:	Sansad Yatra -Hyd-Delhi
28th Apr 2013	:	TJAC Satyagraha Deeksha @Jantar Mantar Delhi for 2 days
29th Sep 2013	:	TJAC Sakala Janabheri Meet @Nizam College
9th Oct2013	:	GoM Committee on Telangana: Cabinet approval on Telangana

2nd Jun2014   :   Telangana declared as 29th State of
                        India.

1.   TDF letters to The President of India, AP Governor, PM
      Madam Smt. Sonia Gandhi / Sri Jaipal Reddy etc.,

2.   Prominent citizens of Hyderabad appeals

3.   My SKC Report

4.   My Resignation as TDF-India President

5.   TDF CII meets

6.   Appeal to STOP Telangana land sales immediately

7.   Press statement on EVM's use in Elections

8.   TDF Membership Drive and Fund raising etc.,

9.   Aluperugani Aajata Shatruvu in Telugu

10.   Personal Details

11.   TDF-India an Overview

12.   Appeal to Prime Minister (PM) Sri Manmohan Singh from
      Eminent Citizens of Hyderabad

7. A STEP INTO OVERSEAS BACK AND FORTH

1) IRAN :

Stayed with a friend in Tehran the capital city of Iran and got a job with a consultant to Iranian Space Research Institute (ISRI), after a month. When I landed in Tehran in March 1976, the Iranians were in happy mood celebrating Nav Rouz (Iranian New Year) and most of the companies were on holiday. I got the job after 3 weeks of my arrival in Tehran.

Looked for better jobs in Iran with my Chemical Engineering and Computer Applications background as Iran was the major producer of Oil and Gas in the Middle East.

Applied to Several Oil / Petroleum Companies and consultants for a suitable job to my background. Oil Service Company of Iran (OSCO) and National Iranian Oil Company (NIOC) were two main producing and exploring companies in Iran and Iran's major income was mainly from Oil Industry only.

As luck would have it, I got a job in OSCO-AHWAZ Oil Feeds South of Iran and joined in Information Services Department. OSCO was operating on behalf of NIOC for Oil exploration, drilling etc., in all over Iranian Oil fields. OSCO is in Iran since 1951 and a major company controlling Iranian politics too.

OSCO had a work force of around 50,000 local Iranians and about 250 foreigners mainly from USA, UK, Holland, Italy etc, representing Global Oil Companies like Mobil, BP, Shell, Agip etc. Only 2 were Asians in OSCO myself D.P. Reddy (Indian) and other one was Mr. Shaikh Zaheer from Pakistan.

OSCO had their own Flights and separate runways, landing and take-off areas and passengers were only OSCO/ NIOC employees, OSCO arranged a seat in their OSCO flight from Tehran to Ahwaz and back for my job interview in Ahwaz H.Q. of OSCO in South Iran.

Had a nice experience and training as well in OSCO Information Services looking after Oil drilling, exploration and distribution etc., using computer application including simulation and optimization methods etc. OSCO had very good facilities for its employees (mainly overseas staff) like furnished accommodation, International School for children, (my daughter Prashanti studied in that school). Hospital, Club, Co-operative Stores, Swimming pool, and play fields like golf etc. We had very pleasant environment with regular get togethers of overseas staff with families.

Also had a very good exposure and had significantly contributed to the company OSCO with my technical Engineering and with Computer Application background and had a very good time with overseas colleagues of different nationalities,

Mr. Reza Shah was ruling IRAN at our time and Tehran was just like any European/ American city with all modern ways of living etc., but Ayatollah Khomeini of Islamic leader wanted to make Iran as an Islamic country and was planning to overthrow Shah of Iran.

Oil Industry strike started in OSCO demanding overthrow of Shah and installing Islamic Republic. In OSCO local employees started strikes to terrorise foreign employees and planned and killed top General Manager (GM) of OSCO whose office was next to my office. From our office we heard the noise and came out to see the G.M. dead. The G.M. was cautious and driving himself instead of engaging driver as he had a threat call from local employees earlier. Military arranged vehicles were taking of security of OSCO offices and residential areas and schools etc., as there was a threat call from Islamic forces.

After murder of General Manager (G.M.), OSCO Managment decided to evacuate all overseas employees including their families to Athens, Greece until normalcy to prevail and get back again to Iran.

We were evacuated from Ahwaz by special flights to Athens, Greece and kept there in 5 star hotels for 3 weeks, expecting normalcy in Oil industry Center of OSCO in Iran. But day by day it was getting worst in Iran and OSCO Management asked to send our families back to their respective countries after 2 weeks.

We were kept 8-10 days more after our families left, but there was no hope of normalcy in Iran, we too were sent back to respective countries and companies.

I came back to Hyderabad - India and gone back to OSCO Ahwaz Iran and OSCO London, UK, to settle my accounts. In Ahwaz OSCO Iranian employees gave me nice farewell with beautiful gifts and I witnessed the Ayatollah Khomeini role in Iran particularly in Ahwaz and Tehran. Similarly gone to OSCO London for my final settlement and also for a suitable job in OSCO Partner Companies in UK, USA, Holland and Italy etc.,

BACK TO INDIA :

Finally returned to India and started a house in the name

of "Pallavi" remembering "Pahllavi" dynasty of Shah of Iran.

While returning form Athens Greece, I had a "Skylab" experience at Bombay Air Port and travelled by train to Hyderabad, as all the flights were cancelled due to "Skylab" threat.

Also admitted our children Prashanti and Vinay in good schools in Hyderabad i.e. St. Ann's High School for Girls, Secunderabad and Hyderabad Public School, Begumpet, Hyderabad.

Again to abroad for work :

I was again in search of jobs in Australia, UK, Middle - East and Africa during my stay in Hyderabad, after return from Iran.

Left for Nairobi, Kenya East Africa with visitor Visa and stayed their local YMCA for some time and later with Mr. Madhav Reddy (Relative) family in their house. Tried for a suitable job in Nairobi for about 2 weeks, but could not get a suitable job in Kenya.

Then flew to Lagos the capital city of Nigeria, West Africa on the same visitor Visa and met an IDPL former employee Mr. Nagaraju Ramaswamy on the flight and he took me to his house directly from Airport for stay in the night. Later moved to Dr. G.V. Reddy's house and Hashem's for staying temporarily searching for jobs in and around Lagos, Nigeria.

Got 2 job offers one in Komplek, Nigeria Limited, Defence Ministry Consultant and another in an University near Ibadan, Decided to join Komplek and gone to India for change of Visa from Visitor to employment visa. Worked in Komplek for about an year and helped the company to get orders from different ministries and also gave contacts in Indian ministries too. My wife Rekha and my son Vinay joined me after moving to Komplek allotted house in Surulere Lagos. Our daughter Prashanti stayed in Hyderabad with our in-laws only to continue her studies in the school.

I got an opportunity to move to INLAKS, a Sindhi Company in their Computer Application Division and worked there for about 6 months.

Again I got a very good opportunity to join a Multi National Company "PRIMLAKS" another Sindhi Company with a Billion Dollar turnover and with 15 companies in Nigeria and another 5 to 6 companies across the Globe with H.Q. in London and other offices in USA, Brazil and INDIA etc.,

My posting was in PRIMLAKS H.Q. in Victoria Island (Lagos) as a Co-ordinator to oversea the day-to- day operations of the group companies like production, inventory, bank transactions, overseas orders and imports etc., and directly reporting to the managing director Primlaks with computerised data and reports etc.,

Interacted with group companies and visited them across Nigeria regularly and getting the information from the managing director of the company and was reporting the same to our group managing director in Lagos.

Also travelled abroad mainly to London the Primlaks H.Q. and was giving the Nigeria group companies performance to overseas H.Q. Also recruited Computer experts from London, UK and INDIA to work with me on day-to-day computerisation and management reports etc.,

Top management of Primlaks was very cordial with their employees and used to organise regular get together for during

Deepavali and other occasions. We had a very good rapport with banks, ministry personnel and Embassy officials as ours was one of the biggest company in Nigeria and whole of Africa. During 1970-1980's only Nigerian Govt. introduced ODD and EVEN number vehicles plying on the road as there was heavy traffic flow form Lagos main land to Lagos Island to attend offices. Nigerians were car pooling to go to offices with odd and even number cars on odd and even number days etc., The big flyover was connecting over the Atlantic Ocean had a very high traffic and some times workers were leaving their homes after breakfast and reaching their offices by lunch time and leaving offices after evening tea and were reaching their homes around dinner time.

We had a fully furnished accommodation and 2 company cars with odd and even number registrations. Driver and servant facility was also provided by the company. There was a big Indian International School in Lagos to serve the education needs of children of Indians.

There was high crime rate in Lagos and other major cities of Nigeria.   The robberies were mainly on the flyovers. When traffic was heavy and robberies usual practice was asking the driver at gun point to handover the car keys and get down; later they were driving the car to the neighbouring country mainly GHANA with new number plates etc., and selling the cars in Ghana's market.

Nigerians were very fond of foreign travel, lavish life style and heavy drinking etc., they were doing these petty robberies mainly during Dec-Jan New Year time to enjoy in London, Paris etc., with the robbed money.

During X-mas season people were thrashing the petty

robbers lynching them openly on main roads (jungle punish-
ment) and beating the culprit to death and leaving the dead
body on the road itself. Some times we used to watch the dead
body for 2 or 3 days also without any police /municipal persons
shifting the bodies from the main roads.

Nigerians were giving good respect to Indians and other
foreigners saying "OYINBO" to any foreigner and greeting
nicely, but get offended if you don't respond to their greetings.

Nigeria is an Oil rich country with virgin lands and good
rains, but due to high corruption and political coups/military
interventions etc., the poor in Nigeria didn't get the fruits of
Nigerian oil economy. Only rich and political leaders benefited
mostly; Hawala transfers were common and Import/Export
companies were using this hawala transactions and were
cheating the public and government.

In Nigeria 50% of the salary amount was allowed to remit
to abroad through banks as your savings. Due to various coups
and political uncertainty and high corruption, the local currency
NAIRA was devalued in comparison to US Dollar and thus our
savings were coming down day-by-day.

So left Lagos Nigeria with family due to the devaluation
and our children's education. Took transfer of residence and
moved most of our belongings with us to Hyderabad.

Our main entertainment and pleasure time was get
together with known families, shopping in super bazaars and
outside beach shops with smuggled goods etc. PRIMLAKS
management was arranging regular get together for employees
with families on Hindu Festivals like Dussehra, Diwali , Indian
Independence day/ Republic Day and Nigerian important days
etc. Indian International School in Lagos was also a meeting
place for all Indians living in Lagos and surrounding areas to
have fun and pleasure.

8. BACK HOME

- After returning to India on the transfer of residence I started a Computer Training and Consultancy Company with another Nigeria returned friend Mr. Satyanarayana., DP Management Services (DPMS) in Hyderabad and gave Computer Training to young students and Consultancy to Banks and other commercial establishments. Computer revolution started in India too at that time and overseas companies preferred Engineers / Graduates with Computer knowledge.

- Being a Chemical Engineer myself, friends and well-wishers advised me to set up a Chemical Industry as Hyderabad is a Hub of Pharmaceutical Industry. In addition to my degree in Chemical Engineering, my experience in IDPL, RRL and Oil Industry Experience in Iran and Nigeria would be helpful in running the industry.

- So, after a thorough search and checking the various options, I had set up Naturite Agro Products (P) Ltd (NAPL) a Solvent Extraction Plant mainly to utilize locally available Raw materials like Chilli and Turmeric. Took my Nigerian returned friends Dr. G. Vallah Reddy and D.V. Janardhan Reddy as Directors in Naturite and me as the Managing Director. Established the unit in the backward area of Ranga Reddy District (near Shamirpet) a backward area even though close to Hyderabad the capital of A.P. as a joint venture. Naturite was established with AP

Industrial Development Corporation (APIDC), A.P. State Financial Corporation (APSFC), and Canara Bank Venture Capital Finance (CVCF), Hyderabad with an investment of Rs. 3.50 crores in 3 ½ acres of land for the manufacture and export of Essential Oils and Oleoresins. Naturite plant was the 1st unit in A.P. to manufacture Spice oils and Oleoresins and Kerala with abundant spices availability was the main center for Essential oils and Oleoresins production.

- Commissioned Naturite plant within a short period 2 years i.e., 1990 to 1992, recruited only local employees to help and assist backward area development.

- Production capacity was 250 metric tons per month of raw material processing for marketing in India and abroad.

- The plant was run with International standards like "Spice House Certificate" and ISO-9000 etc, followed by Central Food Technological Research Institute (CFTRI), Mysore, a CSIR unit like RRL Hyderabad.

- The State Bank of Hyderabad (SBH) provided us the working capital required to run the unit.

- Our competitors were big business/industry people like Synthite, Kancor in Kerala and Sami Chemicals in Bangalore etc.

- As a new entrant to this business, we were exporting our products through these big companies who had a firm footing in the overseas market for spice oils/ oleoresins.

We also produced value-added products like pure capsaicin from Chilies and Curcumin from turmeric for applications in medical and cosmetic industries mainly for exports.

- Due to working capital restrictions, we were operating the plant just at a break- even level only and just sufficient to run the plant.

- Spices Board and Ministry of Commerce, GOI sponsored a trip to East European Countries, Russia, Poland, Hungary and Romania for exploring the market. 5-6 Companies across India including our Company. I joined others in this overseas visit and explored the market for our products.

- Naturite introduced herbal extracts to the Ayurvedic industry and did job work for several companies.

- Aurobindo Industries, Hyderabad showed interest to join us and the Managing Director and others visited our plant and had an MOU with us for financial support as well as Overseas Market support to us.

- Upon Aurobindo's request, we moved to their office in Ameerpet and operated from their premises. To avoid working capital problems for Naturite, Aurobindo cleared our SBH loan completely (about Rs.40.00 lakhs) as part of our MOU.

- Naturite had a minor pollution issue when we were transporting capsicum oleoresin. The product leaked on the road while transporting to Bangalore and caused heavy irritation in the eyes etc., along the road near Ameerpet Hyderabad for about 4-5 kms.

- The Pollution Control Board investigated it and found that our product leaked and caused inconvenience to the public along the road, hence gave a notice to us to shut down the plant. Later, we appealed to them and after a few days, they agreed to restart our production.

- As per our herbal production policy, we did a job work for a Gujarat Company in Ahmedabad. Forest Officials of Maharashtra came and checked the processing of herbals (Gujarati Company) and confiscated the product / RM as the RM was procured unauthorisedly from the forest by our Gujarati suppliers for this job work.

- Similarly, we had a small hitch of pending royalty to our Central Food Technological Research Institute (CFTRI) process to National Research and Development Corporation (NRDC) which was their mistake as we were still not getting any profit in the unit.

- With the above happenings, Aurobindo withdrew from our MOU forfeiting Rs.40 lakhs of the settlement account of Naturite.

- With Naturite, we had enough experience of an industrial operation with problems like strikes, pollution control, technology transfer,and job work issues, etc.

- During this time, we have developed a value-added product Co-Q10 from Solanesol, a tobacco product, which had a very good demand as well as high-value addition.

Tobacco was available plenty in Guntur / Krishna district area.

- To capture this Export market and to come out of our working capital problems etc., contacted Chinese Companies and identified a continuous plant (Swastik Chemicals, Kattedan, Hyderabad) for tobacco processing as our plant was a batch process and arranged to procure enough quantities of tobacco from Guntur area and visited the area and spoke to tobacco growers and merchants etc.

- A Chinese Company came and saw our continuous process and was ready to enter into a market tie-up for 2-3 years for our entire production and they promised to enter into a contract with us after going to China.

- Came out of Naturite forgoing a major share of about Rs 30.00 lakhs in 2006 due to my love for my Telangana. Telangana as I had registered my respect and Love for my Telangana in the 1969 Telangana Movement.

9. "AN EVENTFUL JOURNEY"

For rescheduling my return trip back to Hyderabad, I tried British Airways website online and the system directed me to contact   the agent who booked our tickets. Then only I sent mail to British Airways office to confirm my ticket giving few dates & I wanted to know the availability with the same fare and penalty for date change etc.,

We have checked with BA and other travel agents here. Now, my wife DOMA REKHADEVI REDDY too wants to go with me as the weather is getting cold here and in December getting the seats may be difficult.

So, I requested the Airways to book our two return trip tickets to Hyderabad in BA on any of the available dates: 18th, 19th or 22nd November 2010.

I also mentioned to them that any extra amount to be paid will be arranged.

Due to the time difference between India and USA, we might have not noticed your phone calls as it will be night here.

Finally I had to borrow money from my friend in Hyderabad and managed to reach Hyderabad with greate difficulty. This is how many airlines disserve passengers in the event of passengers getting into difficult situtaion in a strange place.

10. "జనవాక్యం" (Public Applaud)
అలుపెరగని అజాతశత్రువు! – డి.పి.రెడ్డి

రెండు వారాలు ఉద్యమంలో పాల్గొని, తెలంగాణలో తమని మించిన మొనగాడు లేడనుకునేవాళ్లకు ఉద్యమ నాయకత్వాన్ని విమర్శించడమే ఉద్యమం అనుకునేవాళ్లకు ఒక్క కార్యక్రమం చేసి వంద ఫొటోలు, వీడియోలు, మీడియా క్లిప్పింగులు ఫేస్ బుక్కులో షేర్ చేసేవాళ్లకు "ఉద్యమం అంటే ఆచరణ" అని సైలెంటుగా చెప్తున్నాడు డీపీరెడ్డి.

ఆరు పదులు దాటినా ఆ తెలంగాణ ఉద్యమకారుడు అలసిపోలేదు. నాలుగు దశాబ్దాల పైచిలుకు ఉద్యమంలో మమేకమై ఇప్పటికీ తన వయసులో సగం కూడా లేని యువకులను ఉత్సాహపరుస్తూనే ఉన్నాడాయన. పెద్దగా ప్రచార పటాటోపాలు లేకుండానే ఉద్యమ విజయానికి కీలకమైన కార్యక్రమాలన్నెటినో చక్కబెడుతున్న ఆ ఉద్యమకారుడి పేరు దోమ పాండురంగారెడ్డి అంటే అందరికి అర్థం కాకపోవచ్చు కానీ డీపీ రెడ్డి అంటే తెలవని వారు తెలంగాణ ఉద్యమంలో అరుదుగా ఉంటారు. వికారాబాద్ మండలంలోని పాటూర్ గ్రామంలో ఒక మధ్య తరగతి రైతు కుటుంబంలో జన్మించిన డీపీ రెడ్డి కెమికల్ ఇంజినీరింగులో ఎంటెక్ చేశారు.

ఇంజినీరింగ్ విద్యార్థిగా ఉన్నప్పుడే 1969 ఉద్యమంలో ప్రత్యక్షంగా పాల్గొని జైలుకు కూడా వెళ్లారాయన. ఉద్యమం పతాక స్థాయిలో ఉన్నప్పుడు 1970లో మర్రి చెన్నారెడ్డి మేనకోడలు అయిన రేఖ గారిని వివాహం చేసుకున్నారు. ఆ పెళ్లికి చెన్నారెడ్డే పెళ్లి పెద్దగా వ్యవహరించారు. "జై తెలంగాణ" అని ముద్రించి ఉన్న ప్యాకెట్లలో అక్షింతలు ఉంచారాయన పెళ్లిలో.

ఒక బహుళజాతి చమురు కంపెనీలో ఉద్యోగం కొరకు ఇరాన్ వెళ్లారు డీపీ రెడ్డి. ఆయన అక్కడున్నప్పుడే ఇరాన్లో షా ప్రభుత్వానికి వ్యతిరేకంగా తిరుగుబాటు జరుగుతున్నది. దేశమంతా అల్లకల్లోలంగా ఉన్న ఆ పరిస్థితిలో

కంపెనీ వారు డీపీ రెడ్డి కుటుంబాన్ని ఏథెన్స్ కు తరలించారు. అక్కడ మూడు వారాలున్న తరువాత అక్కడి నుండి నైజీరియా వెళ్లారు ఆయన.

మూడు దశాబ్దాల ప్రవాస జీవితం తరువాత 1990లో ఇండియాకు తిరిగి వచ్చి తన స్వంత గడ్డకు ఏదైనా చేయాలనే సంకల్పంతో ఒక ఆగ్రో పరిశ్రమను నెలకొల్పారు 2007లో ఆ వ్యాపారం నుండి వైదొలగి తెలంగాణ డెవలప్మెంట్ ఫోరం (టీడిఎఫ్) ఇండియా విభాగం బాధ్యతలు నిర్వర్తిస్తూ తన పూర్తి సమయాన్ని ఉద్యమానికే అంకితం చేశారు.

ఫొటో: తెలంగాణ మిలియన్ మార్చ్ లో కదం తొక్కుతూ మార్చ్ 2011. టీడిఎఫ్ కార్యక్రమాలను తెలంగాణ ప్రాంతంలో విస్తృతంగా నిర్వహించడంలో డీపీరెడ్డిదే ప్రధాన పాత్ర.

జస్టిస్ శ్రీకృష్ణ కమిటీ వేసినప్పుడు దాదాపు యాభై మంది తెలంగాణ మేధావులను ఒకచోటికి తెచ్చి తెలంగాణకు జరిగిన అన్యాయంపై శాస్త్రీయ ఆధారాలతో కమిటీకి ఒక సమగ్ర నివేదిక ఇచ్చారు. అంతే కాకుండా శ్రీకృష్ణ కమిటీ సభ్యులను స్వయంగా కలుసుకుని తమ వాదన వినిపించారాయన.

ఇక శ్రీకృష్ణ కమిటీ ఒక అన్యాయమైన, తప్పుల తడకల రిపోర్టు ఇచ్చినప్పుడు మరొకసారి ఆ రిపోర్టులోని తప్పులను ఎత్తి చూపుతూ " Justice Srikrishna's Injustice" పేరుతో ఒక పుస్తకం ప్రచురించడానికి చొరవ తీసుకున్నారు డీపీ రెడ్డి. పుస్తక ప్రచురణతో ఆగిపోకుండా ఆ పుస్తకాన్ని ఢిల్లీ వరకూ వెళ్ళి అక్కడి పార్టీ పెద్దలకు స్వయంగా అందజేసి వచ్చారాయన.

శ్రీకృష్ణ కమిటీలోని రహస్య అధ్యాయాన్ని వెలికి తీయడంలో కీలకపాత్ర పోషించి, ఆ అధ్యాయంపై వచ్చిన కోర్టు తీర్పును వెంటనే తెలుగులో ప్రచురించి తెలంగాణలో అందరికీ తెలిసేలా చేశాడాయన.

తెలంగాణ విద్యార్థులకు ఉద్యోగాలు పొందడానికి అవసరమైన శిక్షణ ఇప్పించడంలో, ఉద్యమంలో అరెస్టయిన విద్యార్థులకు బెయిల్ ఇప్పించడంలో, తెలంగాణ ప్రజాసంఘాలవారికి సహాయం చేయడంలో, ఇలా ఢిల్లీ నుండి గల్లీ వరకు ప్రతిరోజూ ప్రత్యక్షంగానో, పరోక్షంగానో ఏదో ఒక కార్యక్రమంలో ఆయన పాల్గొనని రోజు ఉండదంటే అతిశయోక్తి కాదు.

మలిదశ ఉద్యమం మొదలైన తరువాత కరీంనగర్ ఉప–ఎన్నికలు మొదలుకొని, 2009 నుండి ఉధృతమైన ఉద్యమంలోని ప్రతి ఘట్టంలోనూ ఆయన ముఖ్య భూమిక పోషించాడు. అటు జేయేసీ, ఇటు రాజకీయ పార్టీలతో ఎప్పుడూ టచ్‌లో ఉంటూ వివిధ ఉద్యమ కార్యక్రమాలను రూపొందించడంలో తనవంతు పాత్ర పోషిస్తున్నాడాయన.

ఉద్యమ నాయకత్వానికి ఏమాత్రం దగ్గర అయినా, ఆ "అనుబంధాన్ని" ఏదో ఒక విధంగా క్యాష్ చేసుకోవాలనుకునే వారు కోకొల్లలుగా ఉన్న నేటిరోజుల్లో, ఏమీ ఆశించకుండా ఒక సామాన్య కార్యకర్తలా నిబద్ధతతో ఉద్యమంలో పాల్గొనే డీపీ రెడ్డిలాంటి వారు చాలా అరుదు.

నలుగురు కలిసి ఒక ఉద్యమ సంస్థ పెట్టి, నాలుగు రోజులు గడవకుండానే వ్యక్తిగత ఎజెండాలు, అహాల వల్ల అయిదు ముక్కలు అయ్యే నేటిరోజుల్లో, ఇన్నేళ్లుగా తెలంగాణ డెవలప్‌మెంట్ ఫోరం ఇండియా సంస్థను సమర్ధవంతంగా నడపడం ఆయన కార్యదీక్షకు గీటురాయి.

ఒక పార్టీ వారికి కొమ్ము కాయకుండా తెలంగాణ ఉద్యమంలో చురుకుగా ఉన్న రాజకీయ, రాజకీయేతర నాయకులని, సంస్థలనూ నిరంతరం సమన్వయం చేసుకునే డీపీరెడ్డి, మన ఉద్యమంలో ఒక అరుదైన అజాతశత్రువు!

(గత యేదాది "కందెన" పత్రికలో ప్రచురితమైన ఈ వ్యాసానికి కొద్దిగా తాజా సమాచారం జతచేశాను.)

(By: కొణతం దిలీప్)

11. కృష్ణవేణమ్మ కళ్యాణం - రాజకీయత

మహబూబ్‌నగర్ : తెలంగాణ తల్లి ముద్దుల బిడ్డ కృష్ణవేణి వివాహనికి వివిధ దేశాల నుంచి ఎన్నారైలు హాజరయ్యారు. ' తెలంగాణ డెవలప్‌మెంట్ ఫోరం ' తరపున ' డీపీ రెడ్డి ' హాజరై రూ. 10,000 కట్నం చదివించారు. కృష్ణవేణికి ఉన్న తెగింపు మన రాజకీయ నాయకులకుంటే తెలంగాణ ఎప్పుడో వచ్చేదని ఆయన మిడియాతో అన్నారు. ఈ వివాహనికి పలువురు తెలంగాణ వాదులు, జేఏసీ నాయకులు, టీఆర్ఎస్ అధ్యక్షుడు కేసీఆర్, నాగం జనార్ధన్‌రెడ్డి, జూపల్లి కృష్ణారావు తదితర ఎమ్మెల్యేలు, ప్రముఖులు హాజరైన సంగతి తెలిసిందే.

తెలంగాణ కృష్ణమ్మ పెళ్లి మహబూబ్ నగర్ జిల్లా తెలకపల్లి శివగంగా ఫంక్షన్ హాల్లో ఉదయం 10.55 గంటలకు.

– హాజరుకానున్న టీఆర్ఎస్ అధినేత కేసీఆర్, ఎమ్మెల్యే నాగం

– సీమాంధ్ర ప్రలోభాన్ని తిప్పికొట్టిన ఆడబిడ్డ

– తెలంగాణ ఆత్మగౌరవానికి, పౌరుషానికి, పోరాట సంప్రదాయానికి ప్రతీక

– అమరుల ఆత్మలు క్షోభిస్తాయని సీమాంధ్ర పార్టీ సాయం నిరాకరణ

– ఇక ఆత్మబలిదానాలు వద్దని పెళ్లి పత్రికలో పిలుపు

– కొత్త పోరాట రూపాలకు స్ఫూర్తినిచ్చిన కృష్ణవేణి

– ఈ సోయి అందరికీ ఉంటే.... రాదా తెలంగాణ?

– కుహనా నేతలకు కావాలి కనువిప్పు అంటున్న తెలంగాణవాదులు

తెలంగాణ కోసం సాగుతున్న పోరాటం అనేక మలుపులు తిరుగుతున్నది. అనుకోని పరిణామాలకూ దారితీస్తున్నది. అన్ని వర్గాల ప్రజలూ తెలంగాణ సాకారం కావాలని కోరుకుంటున్నారు. కొన్ని స్వార్థ శక్తులు కుత్రపూరితంగా వ్యవహరిస్తున్నాయి. ప్రధానంగా ఈ ప్రజాస్వామ్య వ్యవస్థలో రాజకీయ ప్రక్రియ ద్వారా రూపుదాల్చాల్సిన రాష్ట్ర ప్రక్రియ.... కొన్ని రాజకీయ పార్టీలు.... కొందరు స్వార్థపరులైన నేతల పోకడల కారణంగా ఆలస్యమవుతున్నది. మరోవైపు తల్లి చనుబాల రుణం తీర్చుకోవడానికి

తెలంగాణ బిడ్డలు ప్రాణాలకు తెగించి పోరాడుతున్నారు. ఎంతో భవిష్యత్తున్న యువత రగిలిపోయి, మథనపడి, కళ్లముందు కపట నాటకాలను భరించలేక బాధతో, వేదనతో తనకు తాను ఆహుతవుతున్నది. ఇవన్నీ... తెలంగాణ తెస్తమని, మేమే ఇస్తమని డంబాలు పలుకుతున్న రాజకీయ ఆటగాళ్లకు ఎలా ఉంటుందోగానీ, నిజంగా నికార్సుగా తెలంగాణను కోరుకుంటున్న సాధారణంగా కనిపిస్తున్న అసాధారణ ప్రజలకు మాత్రం తాము చాలా రకాలుగా చాలా చేయాల్సింది ఉ ందని తెలిసొచ్చింది.

కపట నాటకాలకు, కన్నీళ్లకు కరిగిపోవడమూ సరికాదు. ఇంకేమీ కాదంటూ తనువు చాలించడమూ సరికాదని గ్రహించింది తెలంగాణ ప్రజ. అందుకే... ఇన్ని అనుభవాలూ, బలిదానాల తర్వాత తెలంగాణలో కొత్త సోయి మొదలయింది. ఆత్మాహుతులతో సాధించేదేమీ ఉండదు... బతికి చేయాల్సింది ఎంతో ఉందని కొత్త కార్యాచరణకు దిగుతోంది. అందులో భాగమే... పాలమూరు ఆడబిడ్డ కృష్ణవేణి కొత్త పోరాట అడుగు.   కుటుంబ ఆర్థిక స్థితులు ఆమెను నిస్సహాయను చేయలేదు. మీ కుటుంబాన్ని మేము ఆదుకుంటాం.. నీ పెళ్లికి మేము సాయపడతాం అంటూ ప్రలోభపెట్టదలచుకున్న సీమాంధ్ర ఆధిపత్య తెలుగుదేశం పార్టీ ఆటలు ఆమె ముందు సాగలేదు. ఆర్థికంగా లేకపోయినా ఆత్మగౌరవానికి లోటు లేదని, తెలంగాణ పౌరుషానికి కొదువలేదని చాటి చెప్పింది. నా పెళ్లికి సీమాంధ్ర డబ్బులా? అని ఛీత్కరించింది. అమరుల ఆత్మ క్షోభిస్తుందని మనసులో సుడిగుండాలు తిరుగుతుండగా.. టీడీపీ డబ్బుల ప్యాకేజీని తిరస్కరించింది. అదీ.. తెలంగాణ పోరాట చైతన్యం. అంతేకాదు.. తన వివాహ పత్రికనూ వినూత్నంగా రూపొందించింది.

తెలంగాణ కోసం తెగించి కొట్లాడాలని, బతికుండి సాధించాలని, అంతేగానీ ఎంత బాధయినా, ఏ కారణాలనిపించినా ప్రాణాలు మాత్రం తీసుకోవద్దని తన పెళ్లి పిలుపు లేఖలోనే కోరింది. ఆ కృష్ణవేణి పెళ్లి ఆదివారం మహాబూబ్‌నగర్ జిల్లా తెలకపల్లిలో జరుగనుంది. 'ఆత్మగౌరవం కోసం అవసరమైతే ఆస్తులనైనా అమ్ముకుంటాం. సీమాంధ్ర పార్టీలు ఇచ్చే డబ్బులు మాకొద్దు' అని తెగువ

ప్రదర్శించిన తెలంగాణ ఆడబిడ్డ కృష్ణవేణి పెళ్లికి ఆదివారం టీఆర్ఎస్ అధినేత కేసీఆర్ హాజరుకానున్నారు. తెలకపల్లిలోని శివగంగా ఫంక్షన్ హాల్లో ఉదయం 10.55 గంటలకు గౌరారానికి చెందిన బాల్‌రాజుగౌడ్‌తో ఆమె పెళ్లి జరుగనుంది.

సమైక్యవాద పార్టీల చెంప చెళ్లుమనేలా తెలంగాణ తెగువను ప్రదర్శించిన కృష్ణవేణి కుటుంబాన్ని గతంలోనే కేసీఆర్ ఫోన్లో అభినందించడంతోపాటు పెళ్లికి తప్పకుండా వస్తానని హామీ ఇచ్చారు. ఇచ్చిన మాట ప్రకారం ఆదివారం వివాహానికి హాజరై వధూవరులను ఆశీర్వదించనున్నారు. ఎమ్మెల్యే నాగం జనార్ధన్‌రెడ్డి కూడా కృష్ణవేణి తెగువను అభినందించారు. టీఆర్ఎస్, పలువురు తెలంగాణవాదులు కృష్ణవేణి కుటుంబానికి తోచిన రీతిలో సాయమందిస్తున్నట్లు తెలిసింది. మొత్తానికి తెలంగాణ ఉద్యమానికి ఓ కొత్త సంకేతం అందజేసిన కృష్ణవేణి పెళ్లి వేడుకకు ఆదివారం కేసీఆర్‌తోపాటు రాష్ట్ర, జిల్లా పార్టీ నాయకులు, తెలంగాణవాదులు హాజరుకానున్నారు.

తెలకపల్లి, టీ న్యూస్

12. THE FILLIP TO THE MOVEMENT
BY
THE TELANGANA DEVELOPMENT FORUM (TDF) - INDIA

Telangana Development Forum is a (sister concern of TDF-USA) registered in 2007 as a charitable trust to create awareness, networking, training and to set a vision on Telangana Issues.

I was previliged to be the president of TDF- India for a consecutive years serving, sharing, challenging, guiding and participating in the movement for statehood to Telangana in more peaceful but efficient manner.

OBJECTIVES OF TDF- INDIA :

> Provide legal aid to arrested students during Telangana agitation and arrange bails.

> Also gave moral, medical and financial support to the injured students / youth in the Mahaboobabad firing incident.

> Launched "Stop Suicide Campaign" along with other Telangana organizations.

> Submitted a comprehensive report to Srikrishna Committee engaging experts in various fields.

> Prepared a Srikrishna Committee counter Document

> Established Telangana Vision Document.

13. DRIVING TDF ON THE ROAD MAP

Telangana Information Trust : 2nd Saturday meetings from 2006 to 2011 on Telangana-related subjects. Prabhakar. Harinath, Prof Madhusudan Reddy, Ashok, Tippa Reddy.

Telangana Vidyavantula Vedika : All programs /meetings on Telangana: Publication of Books like NEELLU - NIJALU by R.Vidyasagar Rao

Telangana Retired Engineers Forum : Study of Irrigation Projects on Krishna/Godavari rivers mainly Palamoor-Ranga Reddy LI Scheme by visiting the projects with Shyamprasad Reddy, Chandramouli, Penta Reddy, Bheemaiah, Ram Reddy, Ramakrishna Reddy etc.,

Telangana Senior Citizens Association : Collection and publication of T-Martyrs list - 2009 to 2013 by Sreedhara Swami, Ramulu, Somaiah, Eashwaraiah, etc

Telangana Industrial Forum: Working on Telangana Industries including employment for locals etc., - Sudhir Reddy, Gopal, K.Raghu, GS Reddy, Chiranjivi

Telangana Resource Center : Weekly meetings on Telangana from 2011 to 2014; Vedkumar, Someshwar, Neeraja.

Telangana Praja Front : Social and Cultural awakening Gaddar, Vedkumar, Prabhakar. Ch.

Progressive Telangana Foundation / Justice K.M.Reddy Foundation : Vishweshwar R Konda, Vinod B., Kanakaiah R.

Telangana History Society : Telangana History - Capt L.P.Reddy, T. Vivek, Dr. Chiranjivi

T-Advocates JAC : Justice BSReddy, D. Prakash Reddy, Rajendar Reddy, Arun Kumar,G.Mohan Rao, Gopal Sharma, Ramchandra Rao, Satyam Reddy, Prahlad/Legal issues of Telangana

Swagrama Seva : M.Haranath US NRI, Prof. Ramesh Reddy, Prof. Asthana, Vasanth, Srikanth / Encouraging and Making our villages as Model villages

T-Journalists Forum : Pasham, Allam, Tankashala, Srinivas, Shailesh R - Supported TJF financially for important Events.

Dhoom-Dhaam - Andesri, Rasamayi, Goreti, Nernala : Supported in Telangana and sent them overseas to show their talent about T-Culture etc., to our NRIs.

T-Cinema : Rafi, Ramesh, Vijendar R,Mothe, Murali etc., Encouraged our T-Cinema industry as   AP Govt neglecting our artists and only 4-5 families of Cinema Industry are enjoying all the benefits.

T-Rachayithala Vedika : Nandini, Deshapati,Kasula, Sangisetty, Kasireddy, Skybaba - Participated in TRV programs and supported for publishing Books etc.,

TJAC : Prof. Kodandaram, Mallepalli, Raghu, Pittala, Deviprasad, Srinivas Goud, Karam, Vittal, Purushotham , Venkat Reddy, Rajendar Reddy, Sudhir Reddy, Vijendar Reddy etc., Actively participated and supported all TJAC activities

TRS: KCR,Kavitha, KTR, Harish,Nayani, Mahmood Ali,Jagdish R, Vinod B - Supported TRS in all Elections in the name of Telangana.

BJP: Laxman, Kishan Reddy, Ramchandra Rao, Indrasena Reddy, Vidyasagar Rao, Vedire S, Rakesh R, Rajeshwar Rao, Venugopal Reddy ---Joined BJP Programs on Telangana.

CPI: Chada, Narayana, Ramakrishna, Suravarm Supported Telangana issues.

ND: Govardhan R, Pashya Padma

POW: Sandhya, Sajaya

Gulf NRI/Migrant : M.Bheem Reddy, Basanth Reddy, N.Devendar Reddy, Arif.

TAGV: Bal Reddy -He joined many of our programs, like Million March, Rasta Roko etc.,

OUCC: VC OU Ramachandram, Shyam Mohan, Harinath, Guduru, Alumni members - Myself represented on behalf of TDF / Global NRIs in OUCC celebrations.

Legal: Justice BSReddy, Niroop, Prakash Reddy, Mohan Rao, Ramachandra Rao, Gopal Sharma, Rajendar Reddy, Arun Kumar, Sriranga Rao, KK, Satyam Reddy. Took their assistance in Supreme Court cases on Polavaram, etc., students bails and Youth/students cases in courts, etc.,

Minorities: Mahaboob Alam Khan, Zaheeruddin / Siasat, Hameed Mohammad Khan, Arifuddin, Aliyuddin, Maj Quadri, etc., Participated in all their activities including EED Milap, and minority rights activities, etc,.

Dr. MCRCC: Ravindra Reddy, Shashidhar Reddy, Sudarshan Reddy, etc.,

Avayam Trust: Suresh, Dubey, Santosh, etc., participated in and supported in all charity programs to assist students in general and girl students in particular.

Human Rights: Jeevan Kumar : Supported

Forum for Good Governance : Padmanabha Reddy, Chelikani --Joined as a member and supported FGG activities

Dr. Rao's Inner circle: Dr.Panduranga Rao, Narotham Reddy, etc., Interact whenever necessary.

TJS : Kodandaram, Venkat Reddy, Badruddin, Dr. Shankar, Prof. Ramesh Reddy, Sandesh, Avinash, Seshagiri, Dharmarjun, Bairi, Ambati, Pannala, Raman, etc., Part & parcel of TJS and ACTIVE member.

TDF - INDIA : As president TDF-India Represented Global NRIs all over the World from America to Australia i.e., in over 30 countries as President TDF India- Coordinated with NRIs during the T. Movement from 2006 to 2015. Now I am the Chief Advisor to TDF- India and working for the Development of Telangana, the 29th State of India.

14 A PERCIEVED FEAR
In Delhi, The National Capital

PARLIAMENT STAFF ON THE ALERT FOR TELANGANA VISITORS

HYDERABAD: Telangana is now in the suspect list of Parliament as well.   According to sources, visitors from the region are on a high alert list as they are being perceived as a security threat inside the two houses.

In the changed scenario, people from the region who want to watch proceedings from the visitor's gallery are not being granted passes on the basis of a simple recommendation letter from any MP as is the normal practice. Now, the T-MP has to personally endorse the identity of the visitors.

This new practice is the result of the commotion created by the members in the Lok Sabha and the unrest in the region. Parliament security officials have been told to take extra precautions while scrutinizing the T people as there is apprehension that they might create trouble by raising slogans or dropping pamphlets.

" The moment they see a Telugu name or Hyderabad address or recommendation letter from a Telangana MP, officials in the Parliament reception hesitate to issue the pass," said Telangana political JAC member Sri V. Prakash.

Telangana Development Forum president D P Reddy and his three friends also faced a similar problem when they approached the reception officials for passes on March 3, 2011, with a letter from none other than the chairman of the house committee of the Lok Sabha. However, they were denied passes on that date because of intelligence inputs that the Parliament security received about the unrest in Telangana.

Prakash got the entry pass only after the intervention of TRS MP Vijayasanthi the next day. But DP Reddy and his three friends missed the chance of watching KCR and Vijayasanthi disrupting the proceedings and causing adjournments the earlier day because they were denied the passes.

Parliament sources denied having disallowed anybody from Telangana. They, however, admitted that they are keeping track of the people, who want to pay a visit to the visitor's gallery, from the Telangana region. "We have received alert inputs from two regions, one from Uttar Pradesh, and the other from Telangana in Andhra Pradesh," a senior security official of the Lok Sabha told TOI. According to the official, 17 people from Andhra Pradesh were issued passes to the visitor's gallery on Tuesday which included some Telangana people as well.

APPEAL to NRIs to SPONSOR :

Orientation Lectures in Defence / Police Services and Civil Services like IAS/IPS/IRS/IFS etc. in their Native Districts

TDF-India along with Progressive Telangana Foundation [PTF] and Siasat Urdu daily management jointly conducted "Orientation Lectures on Defence / Police Services and Civil Services etc., on 26th Dec'11 at SAP College Vikarabad,Ranga Reddy district.

I had taken the initiative as the native of Vikarabad, Management Committee Member SAP College, Vikarabad and President TDF-India to start this program in Vikarabad 1st and myself bearing all the expenses involved in it. The morning session was well attended by 450-500 SSC/Inter students for Police/Defence careers. There are many vacancies in these sectors and we have to encourage our dropouts from rural youth to join these services for a better future and a disciplined life Siasat organised these Orientation courses in the old City and circulated the job positions available in these sectors some of which are:

1. Central Police Constables [CRPF/BSF/CISF/ITBS etc.,] - - 48,000 vacancies in Southern Command only for SSC students.

2. Police Constables :22,000 vacancies for Intermediate students

3. Police Sub-Inspectors: 2300 vacancies for Degree students.

4. Similarly,there are thousands of vacancies in the ARMY/ NAVY and AIR-FORCE for SSC to Degree students from Jawan to Officer rank. Some how in Telangana,our parents as well as students have apprehensions about ARMED FORCES JOBS, which are actually very good with decent salary and other perks and disciplined life too. WE HAVE TO ENCOURAGE OUR STUDENTS TO ARMED FORCES to serve the country and improve their lives too.

The afternoon session too was well attended with about 300-350 final year degree students for career in CIVIL

SERVICES like IAS, IPS, IFS, IRS etc., There are several job opportunities in AP Transco, APGenco, Excise, Revenue etc., for graduates.

We thank Sri M.Ravindra Reddy SAP College, Vikarabad for allowing us to use the SAP College Gymnasium hall for these orientation courses on 26th Dec'11.

15. TELANGANA DEVELOPMENT FORUM-INDIA (TDF-INDIA) AN OVER VIEW

ABOUT TDF INDIA :

TDF - India, is a sister organization of Telangana Development Forum, USA Inc. (TDF - USA), was registered in 2007 as a Charitable Trust.

OUR ACTIVITIES :

- Create Awareness about Telangana

- Networking of Telangana Organizations

- Impart Training to Telangana Youth

- Create a Vision for Telangana.

- Printed and distributed over Two lakh booklets titled "Andhra Valasa Palanalo Telangana" during 2006 by - elections to Karimnagar Loksabha seat.

- Printed and distributed over 6 lakh booklets titled "Telanganam" (in Telugu, Urdu and English) in 2008 by - elections.

- Distributed copies of Documentary "Still seeking Justice / Nyayam Kosam Nireekshana")

- Printed spirit of Telangana Calendars.

- Issued advertisements in print and electronic media supporting Telangana cause.

- Published and printed publicity material like pamphlets, flexies, banners, stickers etc.

- Assisted NRIs in establishing libraries, community centers, pure drinking water facilities, tree plantations.

- Assisted in distributing scholarships and notebooks to the poor and meritorious students.

- Arranged seminars and workshops by inviting intellectuals, politicians, youth and students to interact on issues concerning Telangana.

- Organised essay writing competitions at school and college level on Telangana topics.

- Conducted career guidance, counseling and soft skills training programs to benefit Telangana students.

- Provided legal aid to arrested students during Telangana agitation and arranged bails.

- Also gave moral, medical and financial support to the injured students / youth in the Mahaboobabad firing incident.

- Launched "Stop Suicide Campaign" along with other Telangana organizations.

- Submitted a comprehensive report to Srikrishna Committee engaging experts in various fields.

PRIORITY :

- Preparing a Srikrishna Committee counter Document

- Prepare Telangana Vision Document.

16. THE ANGUISH IN PRINT - A BOOKLET

LITTLE IDEA! SMALL EFFORT!! BIG IMPACT !!!

We started this Pocket Size Booklet " Andhra Valasa Palanalo.... Telangana" on the injustices done to Telangana in the last 50 years.

It all started with a Little Idea! and we put a Small Effort!!, but the Impact was very BIG !!!

Please read the following few lines to know more on how Little Idea with a Small Effort gave a BIG Impact .

About an year back, as usual we were attending TIT arranged on a 2nd saturday meetings in Hyderabad and were discussing various Telangana related issues. As a moderator of TDF- India group, I was also involved in E-mail discussions on Telangana on TDF - India discussion groups.

While seeing all this, two of my friends from village background [Telangana sympathisers] argued with me that what is the use of our monthly meetings and E- mail discussions as most of the people living in villges are not aware of what we Telanganites were loosing in the unified A.P. We all know that Print and Electronic media are in the hands of Andhras and they were not going to tell our public, what injustices are being done to Telangana and it's people. So, we decided to get more information on the injustices done to Telangana in various fields like Education /Employment, Irrigtion /Water sharing, Medical and Health, language and culture, agriculture /electricity / suicides /migration and Industry and Pollution etc., and wanted to bring a small booklet to educate rural masses in villages.

In this respect, I personally phoned the experts in the field, also sent individual mails and through TDF - India Discuss Programme inviting articles on various topics pertaining to Telangana. [At the end of this mail, I am giving an E- mail of March 22nd 2006 sent to TDF - India group members on this subject for ready reference] .

Some of the prominent experts contacted include:

Prof. Sreedhara Swamy
Prof. Kodandaram
Prof. P. Harinath
Sri. T.Prabhakar Rao
Dr. Revathi
Smt. K.Vimala
Sri Raghava Chary
Sri. Sridhar Deshpandey
Sri. T.Vivek
Sri. K.Penta Reddy
Sri. K.Pratap Reddy
Sri. Pasham Yadagiri
Sri Nandini Sidda Reddy
Sri Deshapathi Srinivas etc.,

It took about 4-5 months to receive and collect some data /information / articles on various topics in the form of hard and soft copies, but it was not complete and many of these articles required translation to Telugu.

As we didn't get full information / data on most of the topics, we started checking the data / information in the existing

T- literature, T- related books and magazines.

We could find some relevant information and statistics on Telangana and with the help of Sunita garu and Vimala garu, collated and arranged them in order in 5-6 sittings. Initially it came nice, but it was very big with more number of pages as we have included history on Telangana and biographies of few prominent People of Telangana.

As our aim was to bring a pocket size booklet for the villagers, on the advice of Sri B.V.Rao garu, we have deleted some pages on T- History and other photos etc., finally came with a nice pocket size booklet on the injustices done to Telangana with about 132 pges. Sri Pasham Yadagiri and S ri Prabhakar Rao have assisted us in checking for the errors / additions / deletions etc., before sending it to the printer.

Meanwhile, KCR resigned and Karimnagar elections were announced in Nov '06; we wanted to test this T- booklet with Karimnagar voters hence it was released by Sri Gaddar in Karimnagar DHOOM - DHAAM on 14th Oct '06. With the assistance of TDF- USA initially we have printed 50, 000 copies and distributed most of them ourselves [TDF - India] directly and some thru TVV, TIT, TRS, T- Students, Sarpanches etc., in all the villages of Karimnagar Prliamentary constituency.

The feed back we received on this T- booklet was excellent and I can confidently say that it influenced many voters including Cong, TDP and BJP party activists to vote in favour of Telangana rather than on party lines. This was confirmed by their leaders; people who were against KCR personally also voted for TRS after reading this booklets. KCR /TRS won this seat with a very comfortable majority of over 2 Lakhs defeating

Cong and TDP eventhough they spent crores of rupees and their leaders /ministers / M.L.A's camped in remote villages weeks together to influence voters. Later, we printed and distributed another 30,000 copies of these T- books in other districts villages through teachers and students. These T- books were going like hot cakes in T- meetings / Dhoom - Dhaam meetings etc.,; but to regret to inform you that only less than 10% we could sell at Rs 5/ each; most of them we gave freely.

Jai Telangana

D.P.Reddy Moderator

TDF - India

TDF-INDIA ACTIVITIES SINCE 2006

To   : All Telangana friends with NRI connections

From   : Telangana Development Forum - India (TDF-India)

Purpose : Membership Drive and Fund Raising

Date   : 11th January 2011

We would like to serve Telangana better through a strong and democratic TDF-India.

We would like to invite thousands of Telangana people to become members and actively participate in TDF-India.

A person of good character with any NRI connection is eligible to become a Member of TDF-India.

NRIS living in other countries can sponsor these Memberships for their relatives and friends in India.

TDF-India, a sister organization of Telangana Development Forum, USA Inc. (TDF-USA), was registered in Secunderabad as a Charitable Trust* with B.V. Rao and D. P. Reddy as the Founder Trustees. They will serve as Chairman and President respectively until a formal organization is installed.

Over the years, TDF-India has undertaken several activities under the direction of TDF-USA with active support of NRIs and local TDF-India volunteers.

TDF-India has been actively participating in all Telangana State related activities from 2004 in alliance with Telangana Vidyavanthula Vedika (TVV), Telangana Employees Association (TEA), Telangana Information Trust (TIT), Telangana Rachayitala Vedika, Telangana History Society, Telangana Retired Engineers Forum, Telangana Senior Citizens Association, Telangana Utsav Committee, and Telangana Joint Action Committee (TJAC) etc.

TDF-India is committed to undertake development projects in Telangana with a view to offer better opportunities for the poor and deserving. TDF-India has realized that this is practical only in a separate State of Telangana. Therefore, we have taken up awareness campaigns to educate the people on the injustices done to Telangana and prepare them to demand a separate state. We have achieved a significant success on this front. A few activities of TDF-India are listed below:

- Brought over 25 Telangana organizations under one umbrella in 2008 on the lines of present TJAC. This has significantly increased mutual cooperation.

- Printed and distributed over 2 lakh booklets titled "Andhra Valasa Palanalo Telangana" in the path-breaking 2006 by-elections to Karimnagar Loksabha seat. Similarly printed and distributed over 6 lakh booklets titled "Telanganam" (in Telugu, Urdu and English) in 2008 by-elections spread all over Telangana to educate rural and urban masses.

- Launched awareness campaign through CDs/DVDs ("Still Seeking Justice"/ "Nyayam Kosam Nireekshana"), pamphlets, flexies, banners, stickers, Spirit of Telangana Calendars, press briefs, advertisements in print and TV media.

- Conducted meetings on every 2nd Saturday on the current topics of Telangana in association with Telangana Information Trust [TIT]. This is an ongoing project.

- Visited irrigation projects on Krishna and Godavari rivers along with Telangana Retired Engineers Forum members to ascertain the status of the projects. Assisted and actively participated in "Pallebata" - an initiative by an NRI from Palamuru in 2008.

- Assisted NRIS in establishing libraries, community centers, pure drinking water facilities, tree plantations and also assisted in distributing scholarships and notebooks to the poor and meritorious students.

- Arranged seminars and workshops including the annual Telangana Pravasi Divas by inviting intellectuals, politicians, youth and students to interact on issues concerning Telangana.

- Organised essay writing competitions at school and college level on Telangana topics.

- Conducted career guidance, counseling and soft skills training programs to benefit Telangana students.

- Provided legal aid to arrested students during Telangana agitation and arranged bails. Also gave moral, medical and financial support to the injured students/youth in the Mahaboobabad firing incident.

- Launched "Stop Suicide Campaign" along with other Telangana organizations to prevent youth/students from taking the extreme step in distress. Instead, encouraged them to work for the movement bravely for the betterment of their lives in future Telangana.

- Submitted a comprehensive report to Srikrishna Committee engaging experts in various fields. This report was commended by one and all. Gave a presentation before the Committee on 7th May 2010.

- TDF-India has started the process of developing a Telangana Vision Document (TVD).

17. THE INCRIMINATION

POLICE COMPLAINT AGAINST THE INCRIMINATION
ABUSIVE ONLINE PROFILES

Telangana activists have lodged a complaint with the Central Crime Station of Hyderabad Police, against a few Facebook profiles and Blogs that have abusive content on Telangana people, culture, statehood movement and leaders.

DP Reddy of Telangana Development Forum India and K. Bal Reddy of Telangana Aatma Gourva Vedika met the CCS police officials today evening and lodged a formal complaint. The complaint made special reference to the Facebook profile of Visalandhra Maha Sabha's leader Mr. Sunkara Venkateshwar Rao.

Mr. Bal Reddy of Telangana Aatma Gourava Vedika informed the media that Mr. Sunkara's Facebook profile contains objectionable comments on the Telangana movement and its leadership. He said "it is a matter of shame that people who masquerade as gentlemen and espouse the cause of a united Andhra Pradesh, stoop to such levels and abuse fellow Telanganites. Their behavior proves the point that the so-called Samaikyandhra agitation is just an Anti-Telangana agitation."

DP Reddy, President of Telangana Development Forum - India warned that this was just the beginning and anyone abusing Telangana people or leadership on social networks would not be spared. He advised youngesters not to spoil their careers by indulging in such useless activities.

The complaint also included a few more Facebook profiles (Like "Dhoma.SivaShankar" and "Telangana. Bidda.92", which are not related to Visalandhra Maha Sabha), which also contain obscene and abusive content against Telangana people, culture, the statehood movement, and also its leadership.

The CCS police informed that they would launch an investigation and people behind these Facebook profiles would be brought to book. Let us all remember that the online world does not give us unlimited freedom. And no one is anonymous online. The same rules and laws that apply in the offline world, apply in the online world too. So, the next time you try to use filthy language on your Facebook profile, think twice!

[img]http://missiontelangana.com/wp-content/

uploads/2013/02/dp-reddy-tdf.jpg[/img]

[i]Photo: TDF - India president DP Reddy speaking to the media in front of CCS after complaining on abusive Facebook profiles.

18. THE PRICKING POINTS FOR THE MOVEMENT.

1. We have participated in all the Bye-Elections since 2006 supporting Telangana only.

2. Briefing US Consulate officials on T-Movement and T-March etc., - 27th Sep'12 at Hotel Fortune Select Manohar Begumpet, Hyderabad.

3. Eminent citizens letter to the President, Prime Minister and Governor of AP.

4. Appeal to STOP land sales around Hyderabad to continue it further on land grabbings.

5. Arranging bail amounts to the arrested students thru Advocates.

6. KCR corrupt projects: Rythu Bandhu, Mission Kakatiya, Mission Bhageeratha, Kaleshwaram Project and other irrigation projects.

7. TDF -USA EVENTS of DC Bathukamma and Dallas convention /Bathukamma in 2010.

8. I had the honor of receiving the TDF-USA "Lifetime Achievement Award" on behalf of Prof Jayashankar Garu @ Telangana Banquet Night on 8th Oct'2010 Dallas Tx USA. Later it was presented to HIM personally on 23rd Jan'2011 at 3rd Telangana Pravasi Divas [NRIday] celebration in NG College Nalgonda!

9. My experience with AP Governor Narasimhan and Anna Hazare in Hyderabad.

10. SKC Report of TDF-India submitted by KCR himself along with TRS Report to SKC in Delhi.

11. Srikrishna's Injustice book by TDF - India on the blunders of SKC Report.

12. SKC Secret /8th Chapter in Telugu submitted all TS MP/MLA/MLCs etc and to General Public/Intellectuals/Journalists.

13. Attended Dialogue on Telangana Meet at CPR Delhi and took DUGGAL Secretary SKC directly on the 8th chapter inclusion by eating dinners with Andhra Leaders in Hyderabad.

14. CM TS KCR garu fully following/adopting the Secret /8th Chapter of SKC after he took over as CM Telangana on 2nd Jun 2014.

15. Agenda for Telangana —submitted to GoM after several discussions with T-Experts on ToR on Telangana etc.,

16. TDF - India 1st Pravasi Telangana Divas [NRI Day] from 2008 OU Hyderabad meeting to 5th PTD in 24th December 2017.

INDUSTRIES & POLLUTION:

The major industries of Telangana like Nizam Sugar Factory, Praga Tools, Azamjahi Mills, DBR Mills etc. were slowly and systematically made sick and were closed, throwing lakhs of workers to the streets. Similarly many of the public sector industries like IDPL, Allwyn, HMT Bearings etc. were also closed down and Andhra rulers conspired to convert them into real estate ventures like malls, hotels etc.

Several Andhra entrepreneurs established Drug and Chemical industries in and around Hyderabad and today almost all the Telangana districts were under the blanket of pollution.

These Andhra entrepreneurs benefitted from the government incentives and entered into FORBES and FORTUNE billionaires list but never preferred locals for employment in their industries. Thus Telangana got a pollution ridden environment in return for the industry-friendly environment it offered. Moreover, with the levels of pollution that exist today and the consequent restrictions Telangana entrepreneurs are deprived of their right to setup industries in their own region even NOW and in FUTURE.

The Musi river which was catering to the drinking water needs before merger got polluted completely with industrial wastes, toxic chemicals etc., all along its way from Patanchervu to Suryapet - a stretch of about 160 kms. Hyderabad a beautiful city with several historical places like palaces, buildings, lakes, gardens and bridges etc., was infact named as Bagh nagar (City of gardens). The Nizam developed (with public money) Hyderabad with cement roads, Road Transport Corporation, Railway lines, Telephone lines, underground drainage system, schools, colleges, universities and Hospitals. Another plus point for Hyderabad is that it had a surplus budget of Rs. 15 crores in 1956.

Hyderabad was the main reason to merge Telangana with Andhra to form Andhra Pradesh in 1956, in the name of common language i.e. Telugu and now in 2009-10 they are opposing the demerger of Telangana citing Hyderabad and its development was by them.

Here's what India Today magazine wrote.

"One of the reasons for the Telangana stir to spin out of control with almost the entire state edging towards near-paralysis was the fear that Hyderabad may be transferred to the new state. Scores of powerful politicians who have sizable business interests in Hyderabad and Telangana, along with real estate sharks allegedly abetted the anti-Telangana fire."

People like Lagadapati Rajgopal were championing the cause of a United Andhra Pradesh because he happens to own the costliest real-estate project in Hyderabad. Similarly several other politicians-turned-businessmen from Seemandhra region who have interests in Power Purchase Hyderabad was after seeing this in all aspects a "Sone ki chidiyan".

19. THE GOOD, BAD AND CHANGING TIMES ABROAD

We were sending /receiving letters through our friends/ contacts who were frequenting India as the postal facility was not good in [IRAN/NIGERIA].

We were going to Telephone Exchange twice, once to inform our Indian contacts about the time/date of call and later speaking to our children who came and were sitting with our relatives in Hyderabad India, etc...

Within IRAN/NIGERIA companies provided us local phones at home and office, but for International calls, we have to go to Telephone Exchanges.

The Postal system was bad in both countries at that time. With Email and Smart phones NOW, it became a Global village i.e., sitting in a remote village also we can speak to anyone across the Globe. India is much better in this aspect.

Whatsapp and Instagrams are popular all over India Now.

Got a phone at my Hyderabad home on a priority basis with my NRI status: similarly got my Housing Board Flat and Two- wheelers to my friends/relatives etc., on a priority basis with my NRI status.

Now our servants, drivers, plumbers, and electricians, etc are having mobile phones and many of them with internet facility, school and college going students are spending most of their time on Smartphones only.

Now, the communication is within our reach at our fingertips. India produces highest number of moible phones in the world after China. From 5.8 crore units in 2014-15 to 31 crore units in 2022-23 locally. In India there are over 1.2 billion mobile phone users and 600 millions smart phone users.

Life in IRAN :

Tehran the capital of IRAN was like any European city with good roads, busses/cars, snow in winter, good super bazars, restaurants and cinema halls, convention centers, etc.,

Many of our Indians who came for Jobs were staying in Youth hostel cooking on gas lanterns meant for room heating and getting naans from nearby shops etc.,

Girls/women were freely going on the roads at midnight too in Tehran.

Iranians give respect to Indians and treating the guests very fondly and nicely.

IRANI CHAI in Hyderabad, Bombay and Lucknow, etc., is different from the original IRANI CHAI of IRAN!. Iranians drink Chai without milk and while drinking they keep a sugar cube in the mouth and gulp the Tea/Chai.

IRAN had very good Airports and OSCO had special flights and separate landing and take-off areas in the Airports of Tehran, Ahwaz and Abadan etc.,

IRAN had a very good infrastructure in the 70-80's only including Offshore /Onshore Drilling sites exporting Petroleum Products Globally and Iran was next to Saudi Arabia in Exports.

D.P.REDDY as I am called by all started in OSCO / IRAN. OSCO had about 50000 employees working out of that about 250 expatriate employees mainly from the USA, UK, Canada, Holland, Italy, etc., Myself [Indian] and Shaikh

[Pakistan] from Asia. My full name DOMA PANDURANGA REDDY was difficult to pronounce for local Iranians as well as expatriates, hence D.P.REDDY came into existence and it was registered in all office registers too.   At that time Sri Late N.Sanjiva Reddy was the President of India: local Iranian colleagues were asking me that am I related to the President of India as my surname too was REDDY.

The same name D.P.REDDY was made popular usage in Nigeria as well as in India too.

I was the President of Telangana Development Forum - India [TDF-India] representing Global NRIs during Telangana Movement from 2006-2014 until TS formation on 2nd Jun'14. Most of the Global NRIs and others know me as D.P.REDDY only and many of them don't know my full name even today!

Life in Nigeria :

Nigeria is the biggest and richest country in Africa with large reserves of Oil & Gas.

Lagos the capital of Nigeria is a developed city with good infracture etc., in the 70-80s only.

Odd and Even number cars were allowed on alterante day on Victoria Island Lagos where the majority of offices (Govt. and Private Corporate etc.,) were there and the Residential area was in the Mainland of Lagos.

PALLAVI - PAHLAVI dynasy of Reza Sha [home name]

Selfmade Man - Left for Iran resigning RRL[GoI] job: Left for Nigeria when Dr. M. Chenna Reddy was the Chief MInister (CM) of Andhra Pradesh (AP) Travel expenses -Took a loan from a friend and returned the amount with interest after a year: A relative from Australia sent 1000/- Dollars for my initial expenses in Tehran, Iran and returned the amount after joining a job in Iran.

Friends in Iran: As I was working in OSCO HQ in Ahwaz, many of our friends were visiting us on weekends and buying their needs from our OSCO society stores at reduced prices.

Friends in Nigeria: Big get-togethers with friends during weekends, visiting local markets for imported goods, etc., : Primlaks was organizing Deewali Mela, Independence Day programs, etc., inviting VIPs to our gatherings mostly in MD's house. Indian School was also a meeting point for Indians on Dasara, School day, etc. Birthday parties and small get-togethers were also common among friends. My 7 BHK house was an ideal place for Birthday parties when Primlaks allotted this house initially: later moved to 3BHK house in the same locality for easy maintenance.

Got Rs 250/- stipend for my M.Tech course in REC Warangal.

After joining IDPL as an Engineer trainee on Rs. 350/- month salary I was sending some amount to my father every month for his expenses and continued the same with my RRL job and overseas jobs etc till his demise in 1996.

Sent money to my close family member to buy a plot in our native place Vikarabad: he bought the plot but in his name. Later I sent money to a friend and he bought the plot in my name: After returning permanently to India, built a house in Vikarabad close to my village.

Under the NRI quota got an APHB flat in Baghlingampally Hyderabad and got a phone connection too to my house under the same NRI quota. Also helped friends and relatives to get 2 wheelers under my NRI quota only.

During my health checkup in London UK (when I was in Lagos with Primlaks) the specialist Doctor confirmed that I have a single kidney only and he took my case file for future reference.

After the 2006 bye-elections onwards Sri K. Chandra Sekhar Rao (KCR), Chief Minister garu was inviting NRIs for lunch regularly and I was co- ordinating with the available NRIs present in Hyderabad and taking them for lunches.Santosh - the present MP Rajyasabha was calling me from 12.00 noon onwards reminding about lunch with KCR : he was receiving us and was helping KCR in getting food etc., to the dining table.

CM KCR took me and Madhu K Reddy US NRI to Pragathi Bhavan for lunch on 11-3-2015 from the CII meeting at Taj Krishna Hyderabad: it was the last interaction with KCR after TS formation.

20. THE UNDEMOCRATIC DEMOCRACY

THE GOVERNANCE IN TELANGANA POST SEPARATION :

After the bifurcation of Andhra Pradesh into A.P and Telangana driven by the spirit of Sri Prof. Jayasankar Sir, supported by Sri Prof. Kodandaram who moved student and youth community and under the leadership of Sri Kalwakuntla Chandrasekhar Rao the separate statehood for Telangana has become a reality. The self esteem of Telanganites has been restored and the people of Telangana were jubilant.

Unfortunately the blues of freedom and happiness was short lived. The first Chief Minister of Telangana, although started of well by announcing several people welfare schemes. When it. came to implementation, most schemes were given to the Chief Ministers' kith and kin and people continue to starve. State resources and revenues were syphoned to the CM' family and only the CM' wealth grew multifold. Common telanganite life changed nothing. The CM never attended his office, assembly and was absolutely unaccessible to his fellow ministers, beaurocrats, media and general aggrieved citizens.

This kind of unbridled freedom transformed KCR a tyranny, dictstorship and political arrogance. The people of Telangana understood the level of corruption by KCR and rooted him out of power in 2023 assembly polls reducing to a just infamous MLA.

The second Chief Minister of Telangana is a congress politiciain Sri Revanth Reddy. Experienced, aggressive, a team player and courageous leader. Time will prove the future of Telangana.

21. PERSONAL EXPERIENCE OF ANARCHY

- Bought a plot of 1000 yards in a venture along with other relatives / friends in 1979 at Banjara Hills layout of 14 acres area before I left for Nigeria by paying Rs 19000/-.

- It was lying idle & neighbors of the MLA colony grabbed 6 acres of our venture land unauthorisedly in 1990's.

- In 2016 November applied for clearing our plot under the LRS scheme of TS Govt by paying Rs 5.00 lakhs and Rs 10000/- processing fee. My friend V.Malla Reddy too applied under this LRS scheme in the same venture by paying Rs 4.00 lakhs [800 yards] and a processing fee of Rs 10000/- along with me.

- The LRS was not cleared for our plots till Aug 2020 Malla Reddy expired on 25th Aug 2020 due to ill health in Corona times.

- As on 14th December 2020 there were 25 Lakhs LRS applications were pending in the state and over 4.00 lakhs in GHMC itself. TS Govt is not acting even under High Court strictures on LRS and plots registration.

- After returning from Nigeria bought 15 acres of land in Advimasjid adjacent to Narayanpur village in the year 1990 and gave this land as a Mortgage to SBH for the working capital loan to our industry Naturite Agro Products Ltd which was a joint venture unit with APIDC/APSFC. Did agriculture activities in the land with several crops and orchid with

Mango and Guava trees etc., For my 15 acres land, it was finally approved after my one year struggle by contacting MRO, Dy. Collector and Collector etc.

One of the corrupt practices of AP / Telangana politicians and MLAs has been to land grabbing and use their power to get those lands registered on thier name or there Kith and kin.

All possible efforts were made by me using my contacts and legal standing but invain. This is the case with hundreds of people like me who are helpless and put to hardship by power politics and ignore activities of our people representatives. This is one of the major income source for the grabbers since the price of the land is ever increasing.

This is just a tip of the ice berg pertaining but there are several thousand of such cases unresolved as victims left hopes any more.

Even God's endowment lands of 23000 Acres were illegally encroached but no action been taken although this is a state issue.

22. THE VOICE OF YOUTH
'యువ గళం'
యువతలో తీవ్ర వ్యతిరేకతకు కారణాలు

1) లక్ష ఉద్యోగాలు ఇవ్వనందుకు

2) గ్రూప్ వన్ పరీక్షలు ఒక్కసారి కూడా పెట్టనందుకు..

3) కాంట్రాక్టు ఉద్యోగస్తులను పర్మినెంట్ చెయ్యనందుకు..

4) కౌలు రైతు రైతే కాదు అన్నందుకు..

5) ప్రశ్నించే గొంతు నొక్కేస్తున్నందుకు..

6) ప్రజల హక్కులు కాలరాస్తున్నందుకు..

7) మీడియాలో ఏ వార్త రాకుండా చేస్తున్నందుకు..

8) సమస్యలపై ఉద్యమిస్తే పోలీసులచే అణచివేతకు గురి చేస్తున్నందుకు..

9) అక్రమ కేసులు పెడుతున్నందుకు..

10) ప్రతిపక్షాలను లేకుండా చేస్తున్నందుకు..

11) ఉద్యమకారులను పట్టించుకోనందుకు..

12) టిఆర్ఎస్ నాయకులు భూకబ్జాలు పెడుతున్నందుకు..

13) రామోజీకి భూమి ఇచ్చినందుకు..

14) బాలకృష్ణ సినిమాకు వినోదపు పన్ను మినహాయింపు ఇచ్చినందుకు..

15) బాలకృష్ణ దవాఖానాకు ఆరుకోట్ల పన్ను మాఫీ చేసినందుకు..

16) ఆంధ్రా కాంట్రాక్టర్లకే పనులు ఇచ్చినందుకు..

17) ఉద్యమద్రోహులకు పదవులిచ్చినందుకు..

18) ఆరోగ్యశ్రీలో కరోనాను చేర్చలేక పోయినందుకు..

19) ప్రైవేట్ దవాఖానాలు దోచుకుంటున్నా పట్టించుకోనందుకు..

20) పేదలకోసం తెచ్చిన కేంద్ర ప్రభుత్వ పధకం 'ఆయుష్మాన్ భారత్' ను తెలంగాణల అనుమతించనందుకు..

21) కేంద్రం ఇచ్చిన కరోనా పైసల లెక్క చెప్పనందుకు..

22) మాటలతో ప్రజలను మభ్య పెడుతున్నందుకు..

23) తెలంగాణ ముఖ్యమంత్రివై ఉండి రాయలసీమను రతనాలసీమ చేస్తా అన్నందుకు..

24) దళితులకు మూడెకరాల భూమి ఇవ్వలేకపోయినందువలన..

25) **LRS** తో ప్రజలను ఇబ్బందులకు గురి చేస్తున్నందుకు..

26) ఇచ్చిన హామీలను నిలుపుకోలేకపోయినందుకు..

27) మీరు చెప్పేదొకటి చేసేదొకటి కావటం వలన..

28) ఆరేండ్ల తరువాత ఇప్పటికీ గత పాలకుల పాపం అని అనటంవలన..

29) జర్నలిస్టులకు ఇండ్ల స్థలాలు ఇస్తానని ఇవ్వకపోవడం వలన..

30) మీ మంత్రులు తలా ఒక మాట తేడాగా మాట్లాడటం వలన..

ఇంకా అనేక కారణాలవలన యువత మీకు వ్యతిరేకంగా ఉన్నారు సార్ నమస్తే.. కపిలవాయి బిరవీందర్...

23. MY RESIGANATION AS PRESIDENT TDF - INDIA :

For over 9 years since 2006 B.Venkateshwara Rao (B.V.Rao) garu as Chairman and myself as President TDF-India worked all these years in the T-Movement along with TJAC and other T-Organizations like TVV,TREF, TIT,TSCA, TAGV and many more.

Now, we are in our own State which we got after 6 Decades of struggle and several hundreds of sacrifices. TDF-India is well known all over Telangana State due to our sincere efforts of educating the masses as well as our leaders on the injustices done to Telangana and why we need our own State. TDF - India has to Play an ACTIVE Role in the Development of TS to make it a MODEL State in India.

Earlier, in 2011 Dallas Convention only,I had asked Viplav and Madhu to look for another young person in my place in TDF-India: later in 2012 told the same to Murali when he attended TDF-India meeting in Tarnaka office. They asked me to continue some more time to work with TJAC as I have a good rapport with TJAC and good contacts with T-Organizations etc.,

After TS formation,TDF -India organized a SEMINAR on 30th August 14 on "TDF and TS Development" inviting TS Ministers /Advisers along with TJAC Members and available TNRIs. In that meeting,it was decided to Restructure TDF-India by inducting Young Activists from all T-Districts as well as representatives from Global TDF Chapters etc.,. But some how,

TDF parent Organization TDF-USA didn't take any Action and hence TDF-India continuined as it was.

Meanwhile, I Reminded Dr. Gopal Reddy garu, Madhuji and Purushothamji in CII/TDF Meet on 30th Jan'15 and later Madhuji on 11th March 15 at CII Meet, and during personal discussions also similarly, I was discussing this Issue with our TDF-India Chairman Sri BVRao garu too on regular basis.

Then I suggested TDF -USA Board to RELIEVE me as TDF -India President Immediately and REPLACE it with an Young and Active Person as soon as possible.

I placed on record my sincere thanks, appreciation and gratitude to TJAC Chairman Prof M.Kodandaram and other TJAC Members also for their Encouragement and support.

24. MY FANGLED EXPERIENCE IN NEW YORK USA

I wish to share one of my nightmarish incidents that happened on an overseas trip in the most developed country like the US. My experience of how I managed the episode with no money, no passport, no flight tickets, no place to stay as my briefcase was stolen in a fraction of second. My story will be a textbook lesson for the new generation who are normally casual .

I was. working with a leading and highly reputed company in Nigeria , PRIMLAKS logos. It was in the 80s. I was on a business trip to Seattle, Washington for two weeks.. After successfully completing my work,. I booked my return ticket to Nigeria, via Newyork where I had a transit stay.

My friends and colleagues in Nigeria advised me to be careful in Newyork down-town as there were many incidents of robberies / cheating cases . I took my return flight from Seattle to Lagos with a stop-over in Newyork. I had already.

I reserved a 5-star hotel near NYC airport for my transit stay for a few hours: Upon arrival in NYC , I took a taxi directly to the reserved hotel, the " Best Western Hotel" .

Reception at the hotel asked me to fill the guest form with my personal & travel details etc.,..To write my details which is mandatory for all the guests. I kept my briefcase on the floor beside me close to my feet and completed the guest details & handed it over to the Receptionist. To my utter surprise ,I didn't find my briefcase after handing over the filled form to the receptionist: it was just a few seconds only. I immediately reported to the receptionist about my missing briefcase in which my passport,money clothing, flight tickets etc were there. I was almost devastated. Losing a passport in a foreign country while on travel is nothing short of a hell. The receptionist told me to check in the washrooms as someone might have taken my briefcase by mistake or unknowingly. I had gone & checked the wash rooms ,but could not find my briefcase & informed the receptionist.

The hotel staff then called the police & informed them about the missing briefcase in front of the Reception desk only . After 5-10 minutes a big police vehicle came with a high volume siren & a police woman got down & entered the hotel lobby. She enquired about the missing item with the hotel reception & other staff, then talked to me too. She made 2-3 phone calls to whom I do not know but told me that "Mr Reddy you forget about your briefcase now" ,if you are lucky the thief may throw it [your briefcase] in a dustbin after taking away the cash & other valuables. Anyhow, I am giving you the FIR file number now, which you can submit in your embassy to get a new passport for you .

Then I asked the hotel manager to allow me to spend this night in the hotel lobby as I don't have money and passport too : but they were unkind and outrightly refused and asked me to vacate the place.

I called my two B.Tech classmates in NYC & DC on call collect system [Receiver will pay the telephone bill of the caller after identifying the caller] available at that time as I didnt have money with me: but both of them were out of station on tours . Also called our PRIMLAKS Miami USA office ,but nobody lifted the phone as it was evening & the office was closed. Luckily, before leaving Lagos,I had a printout of my US contacts list with me in my coat pocket.

Later,I made another call on call collect system to my uncle

NNReddy in Chicago & he immediately contacted one of our relatives who was working in Columbia University NYC & told him about my unforeseen situation and asked him to take me to their residence...My relative came after an hour or so & picked me up from the hotel and took me to his place.

Comfortably stayed with my relatives for the night but I was in a helpless and hopeless condition mentally.

My relative dropped me off at a metro station near the Indian Embassy and then proceeded to the Indian Embassy and explained my missing briefcase & showed the police FIR to the staff there. One of the staff members told me to prove my identity and said how do we recognize you as an Indian as many Srilankans & others came to the Embassy claiming as Indians. Then ,I got upset & angry and asked the staff to call a Senior officer or Commercial attache/Ambassador to come and talk to me.

One senior manager, Sardarji , came & asked me what was the matter?. I told him all about missing briefcase in which I had my passport also told him that I am working with PRIMLAKS a multi-national company in Lagos.You can speak to your Ambassador there in Lagos ,Nigeria who knows about our company & I met him in our company get-togethers like DIWALI MELA etc.,. Sardarji got convinced about my narration and nativity & asked me to bring 2 PP size photos & fill the form with personal details & collect the Passport in the afternoon.

I Went out and brought 2 PP photos [paying US $10.00] and submitted them to the embassy along with my personal details. Now it is the issue of my Nigerian Visa to enter the country.

Approached the Nigerian High Commission for my VISA to

Lagos & explained to the senior staff there about my company in Lagos PRIMLAKS & my missing briefcase with my passport in it etc., & he asked me to come with my Passport & they will endorse Nigerian VISA immediately.

My next visit was to British Airways for a flight back to Lagos Nigeria. I had the counterfoil of my 1st class British Airways ticket in my coat pocket which helped me to counter check my travel itinerary etc,.The British Airways staff were very cordial & really understood my delicate problem & promised to confirm my ticket back to Lagos for tomorrow as the Lagos time is night now [US time] .

In the afternoon ,I collected my Passport from the Indian Embassy NYC & also collected my return confirm bag and never leave it in the hotel locker or room.

Before you leave for your overseas trip, make a few copies of your passport, flight tickets and place them in 3 or 4 locations in the suitcase. One set of leaves with your wife and one with the office.

When men change the dollars to local currency, don't leave your belongings on the trolley unattended. There is a tie-up between robbers and bank employees.

If you are heading to a country for an official meeting, don't plan any sightseeing trip to any other country just because it falls on the way. If there is any mishap like this, you will miss your meeting.

Keep all contacts with you of all your acquaintances. Eat less during flight. Keep all your medicines handy and adequate.

Keep a pen. Begging pen from others to fill up immigration forms is not decent.

THE MOST FORMIDABLE TRIO WHO BROUGHT FREEDOM TO TELANGANA

Smt. SONIA ji who has seen the agony of death moved emotionally and with a pinch of guilt on Youth immolations and killing and conceded in favour of a separate statehood to Telangana.

KAKATIYA MEMORIES WARANGAL FORT

తెలంగాణ తల్లి

Sri K. Chandra Sekhar Rao
The 1st Telangana State Chief Minsiter - KCR

తెలంగాణా రాష్ట్ర ప్రథమ ముఖ్యమంత్రిగా శ్రీ కె. చంద్రశేఖర రావు, 2వ జూన్ 2014న అధికారం చేపట్టాడు. ప్రజాసంక్షేమ పథకాలు ప్రవేశపెట్టినా అవి ప్రజలకు బదులు తన వారికి మాత్రమే లభింపచేసి, స్వార్థపరుడై, అవినీతిని పోషించి, నిరంకుశుడై, కుటుంబపాలన, నెపోటిజం, రాజ్యాంగ వ్యతిరేక కార్యక్రమాలతో అప్పులతో కూలిపోయిన ప్రజాపాలనతో ప్రజా చైత్యన్య శక్తికి తలవొంచి 2023 అసెంబ్లీ ఎన్నికలలో పదవీచ్యుతుడైనాడు.

జననం : 17 ఫిబ్రవరి 1954 (వయస్సు 69 సంవత్సరాలు),

చింతమడక.

పార్టీ : భారత రాష్ట్ర సమితి

జీవిత భాగస్వామి : శోభారావు (మ. 1969)

మనవలు : అలేఖ్యరావు, హిమాన్షు రావు, దేవనపల్లి అనిల్ ఆదిత్య, మరికొందరు

పిల్లలు : కె.టి. రామారావు, కె. కవిత

స్థాపించిన సంస్థ : భారత రాష్ట్ర సమితి

అవార్డులు : ఇండియన్ ఆఫ్ ది ఇయర్ పాపులర్ ఛాయిస్ అవార్డు.

అన్నమల రేవంత్‌రెడ్డి (జననం నవంబర్ 8, 1969) భారత జాతీయ కాంగ్రెస్‌కు చెందిన రాజకీయ నాయకుడు. విద్యార్థిగా ఉన్నప్పుడు ఏ.బి.వి.పి.లో సభ్యుడు. 1992 లో 24 ఏళ్ళ వయస్సులో పెళ్ళి చేసుకున్నారు. తర్వాత 2004 లో టి.డి.పితో రాజకీయ ప్రస్థానం ప్రారంభించారు. 2008 లో స్వతంత్ర అభ్యర్థిగా శాసన మండలి సభ్యుడిగా ఎమ్మెల్సీగా ఎన్నికయ్యారు. అనంతరం టి.డి.పి. అధినేత ఎన్. చంద్రబాబు నాయుడుతో సమావేశమై తెలుగుదేశం పార్టీలో చేరారు. 2009లో కొడంగల్ నియోజకవర్గం నుంచి 46.45% ఓట్లతో ఆంధ్రప్రదేశ్ అసెంబ్లీకి ఎన్నికయ్యారు. తన మొదటి పదవీ కాలంలో కోసిగి బస్ డిపో మరియు పాలిటెక్నిక్ కళాశాల నిర్మాణాన్ని ప్రారంభించారు.

2014 సార్వత్రిక ఎన్నికల్లో మరోసారి పోటీచేసి కొడంగల్ నియోజకవర్గం నుండి 14,614 ఓట్ల మెజార్టీతో తెలంగాణ అసెంబ్లీకి ఎన్నికయ్యారు.

తెలంగాణ శాసన సభలో తెలుగుదేశం పార్టీ ఫ్లోర్ లీడర్‌గా ఎన్నికయ్యారు. 25 అక్టోబర్ 2017న రెడ్డి భారత జాతీయ కాంగ్రెస్‌లో చేరే ఆలోచనలో ఉన్నట్లు నివేదికలు వెలువడిన తర్వాత, తెలంగాణ టి.డి.పి నాయకుడిగా రెడ్డిని తొలగిస్తున్నట్లు టి.డి.పి. ప్రకటించింది. సెప్టెంబర్ 20, 2018 న తెలంగాణ ప్రదేశ్ కాంగ్రెస్ కమిటీ ముగ్గురు వర్కింగ్ ప్రెసిడెంట్లతో ఒకరిగా ఎన్నికయ్యారు. తెలంగాణ సి.ఎం. గా రేవంత్‌రెడ్డి ఆరు ఎన్నికల హామీలను ఆమోదించారు.